FLOYD CLYMER'S MOTORCYCLIST'S LIBRARY

The Third Book of the
VESPA

A Practical Handbook covering all models 1963-1972 (except GS and SS models)

John Thorpe

ANNOUNCEMENT

By special arrangement with the original publishers of this book, Sir Isaac Pitman & Son, Ltd., of London, England, we have secured the exclusive publishing rights for this book, as well as all others in THE MOTORCYCLIST'S LIBRARY.

Included in THE MOTORCYCLIST'S LIBRARY are complete instruction manuals covering the care and operation of respective motorcycles and engines; valuable data on speed tuning, and thrilling accounts of motorcycle race events. See listing of available titles elsewhere in this edition.

We consider it a privilege to be able to offer so many fine titles to our customers.

FLOYD CLYMER
Publisher of Books Pertaining to Automobiles and Motorcycles
2125 W. PICO ST.   LOS ANGELES 6, CALIF.

INTRODUCTION

Welcome to the world of digital publishing ~ the book you now hold in your hand, while unchanged from the original edition, was printed using the latest state of the art digital technology. The advent of print-on-demand has forever changed the publishing process, never has information been so accessible and it is our hope that this book serves your informational needs for years to come. If this is your first exposure to digital publishing, we hope that you are pleased with the results. Many more titles of interest to the classic automobile and motorcycle enthusiast, collector and restorer are available via our website at www.VelocePress.com. We hope that you find this title as interesting as we do.

NOTE FROM THE PUBLISHER

The information presented is true and complete to the best of our knowledge. All recommendations are made without any guarantees on the part of the author or the publisher, who also disclaim all liability incurred with the use of this information.

TRADEMARKS

We recognize that some words, model names and designations, for example, mentioned herein are the property of the trademark holder. We use them for identification purposes only. This is not an official publication.

INFORMATION ON THE USE OF THIS PUBLICATION

This manual is an invaluable resource for the classic motorcycle enthusiast and a "must have" for owners interested in performing their own maintenance. However, in today's information age we are constantly subject to changes in common practice, new technology, availability of improved materials and increased awareness of chemical toxicity. As such, it is advised that the user consult with an experienced professional prior to undertaking any procedure described herein. While every care has been taken to ensure correctness of information, it is obviously not possible to guarantee complete freedom from errors or omissions or to accept liability arising from such errors or omissions. Therefore, any individual that uses the information contained within, or elects to perform or participate in do-it-yourself repairs or modifications acknowledges that there is a risk factor involved and that the publisher or its associates cannot be held responsible for personal injury or property damage resulting from the use of the information or the outcome of such procedures.

WARNING!

One final word of advice, this publication is intended to be used as a reference guide, and when in doubt the reader should consult with a qualified technician.

Preface

LOOKING at the clean lines of the Vespa, it is hard to believe that the basic design of this up-to-the-minute machine was laid down over twenty-five years ago. Yet that is a fact, and it speaks volumes for the soundness of the original concept that its makers have not found it necessary to depart from it. The combination of a monocoque chassis/body unit; trailing-link front fork and swinging-arm rear suspension incorporated in a side-mounted engine/transmission unit has more than stood the test of time. It has triumphed to such an extent that the Vespa today is perhaps *the* prime example of a ubiquitous and truly international vehicle.

It is so enclosed and compact that one is perhaps entitled to feel dubious about attempting anything more than cleaning and adjusting. Well, thanks to its in-built reliability it will thrive on that—and no more—for thousands of miles. But the time *will* come when it needs at least a decoke, if not a complete overhaul.

That's where this book comes in. I have tried to make it as informative as possible without becoming too technical. In the chapters on more advanced mechanical work, I have set the various stages out step by step, and these have been reinforced by exploded drawings showing the inter-relationship of the various parts. I have, quite deliberately, avoided annotating these. If you already know what the parts are, you don't need me to tell you. If you don't, then the visual reference is more valuable than a list of names; and I have chosen to make the illustrations big enough for each part to be picked out with ease.

It's an experiment—and I think the answer we've come up with is the right one for the majority of Vespa owners.

You can apply the information in this book to all Vespas (except the GS and SS models which are dealt with in *The Book of the Vespa GS and SS* in this series) built since 1963. But if you have never tackled home maintenance before don't be carried away by enthusiasm and strip the engine here and now. Do only the jobs that obviously need to be done—and gain experience on the simple ones first. And one further point—never use "rogue" spares, even if they are cheaper. Always buy genuine Vespa spares through an accredited dealer. That way, you're sure of what you're getting and your Vespa will continue to serve you well, both as a fun machine and a workaday runabout. Good riding!

JOHN THORPE

The Vespa 90

The Vespa 90 SS

The Vespa 125 Primavera

The Vespa 150 Super

Contents

1 What it needs	1
2 Background for beginners	3
3 Don't forget your tools	15
4 Put method in your maintenance	18
5 Be your own doctor	21
6 Engine removal and strip	28
7 Carburettor service	38
8 Care of the electrics	42
9 Suspension, brakes and controls	55
10 On the road	66
Appendixes	
1 Data	74
2 Roadside troubles	76
Index	81

1 What it needs

SCOOTERS as we know them are a post-war innovation—but they were in fact the realization of a dream of long ago. Ever since the turn of the century motor-cycle manufacturers had tried again and again to produce a machine which would combine at least part of the weather protection of a car with the handiness of the two-wheeler. And again and again they failed —beaten by handling problems, cooling problems, or structural problems.

It took about fifty years before an Italian aircraft firm came up with all the right answers—and then only as the result of some extremely accurate bombing by the Royal Air Force who had half-wrecked the Piaggio factory at Pontedere and left the staff with a number of headaches. Not least of these, paradoxically, was sore feet! The usable parts of the works were few and far between, and getting from one to another was a tiring and timewasting business. To cut down the footwork, Piaggio designed a little two-wheeled runabout with a 98 c.c. engine, an open footboard, and a small front shield. It was, in fact, the prototype of the Vespa scooter —and with aircraft soon out of the running as salesware it didn't take Piaggio long to realize that this diminutive vehicle might provide them with a living once the war was over.

It did. Right from the time of its appearance as a commercial proposition in 1946—with the capacity upped to 125 c.c.—the Vespa sold. It is still selling, and outwardly it is not much changed. Inwardly, though it's another matter. The machine has been refined out of all recognition.

With refinement has come the sort of day-in day-out reliability that a machine meant to work for its living has got to have. Your Vespa does not need much in the way of major overhauls—but it does like a regular "decoke." At long intervals, you may need to overhaul the clutch, too. This is another fairly simple job providing it is properly tackled. And after a very considerable mileage the engine bearings will need renewal. Here, the work is more complicated, calling for some mechanical skill, of course, and a reasonable tool kit.

All the rest of the work on a Vespa engine/transmission unit is more complicated, so I have largely confined myself to describing jobs which the great majority of riders can tackle. I've outlined the major ones, too for the benefit of knowledgeable riders who wish to go further, but it must be stressed that you will need more than the average degree of experience and mechanical ability to undertake such work. Remember, the main attraction of doing jobs yourself is to save either time or money. You'll save neither if you get out of your depth.

All work on the scooter must, of course, be carried out very carefully indeed. This is not a machine in which a proprietary engine has been tacked into a frame dreamed up by a snake-charmer and linked to the rear wheel by whatever length of chain happened to fit. There have been machines like that—I've ridden some!—but definitely not Vespas. Every part of your machine is designed to match its neighbour exactly, and there has been no compromise at all in making the layout right for the job it has to do.

So, before you start work on the machine study the relevant chapter thoroughly, until you have the sequence properly memorized. Don't work on a dirty unit, and don't use any but the proper spanners for the job.

Remember, too, that there is an art even in the simplest of tasks. Every spanner is made of a length which, when hand pressure is exerted at the other end, gives just the right leverage to do up a nut or bolt of the appropriate size. Thumping the spanner round with a hammer or trying to increase the leverage by linking two open-enders together will strain or strip threads, and may snap studs or bolts in half—to say nothing of wrecking the spanners. Therefore, beware of over-tightening. It is sufficient if a nut is turned down hard enough to lock a spring washer fully.

Of the routine jobs you will be carrying out, the most important are those on the braking system. Keep a careful check on your brakes and don't take them for granted. Every day they lose just a little of their stopping power as the linings gradually wear a fraction of a thou. more.

The answer is to test the brakes at least once every week by adopting the "task" system of maintenance I've outlined in Chapter 4. This has been evolved to ensure that every important adjustment is checked so frequently that failure from neglect is almost impossible. The cost in time is negligible —yet it may save you many pounds in hard cash.

2 Background for beginners

ALL Vespas have two-stroke engines—the simplest form of power unit and, in the opinion of many of us, also the best. A two-stroke comprises just three moving parts. They are a pair of flywheels carried on shafts which revolve in bearings set in the crankcase; a connecting rod mounted on the crankpin joining the flywheels; and a piston—carried on the connecting rod—that moves up and down in a cylinder bolted to the crankcase. As the piston reciprocates, it moves the connecting rod, which in turn drives the flywheels. The piston travel from its uppermost point (Top Dead Centre—usually abbreviated to TDC) to its lowermost point (Bottom Dead Centre, or BDC) is called "the stroke."

Petrol/air mixture is sucked into the crankcase through an inlet port as the piston travels up the cylinder. In some Vespas this port is opened and closed by the lower edge of the piston (Fig. 1). In others, a cutaway section in one of the flywheels acts as a rotary valve. As the piston descends, this mixture is compressed and is then pumped into the cylinder through another set of piston-controlled ports known as "transfers." Yet another port connects with the exhaust system, allowing burned gases to escape from the cylinder.

The beauty of a two-stroke is that every time the piston reaches the top of its travel the engine fires. There is consequently one power impulse to every revolution of the flywheels, giving an output as smooth as that of a twin-cylinder four-stroke. And the four-stroke would have at least thirty moving parts—ten times as many as the two-stroke requires!

How is this near-miracle achieved? Imagine a two-stroke engine in which the piston is at BDC after a power stroke. At just this moment the last remnants of the burnt gas are still streaming out of the exhaust port in the base of the cylinder, and two streams of fresh gas are entering through the transfers. These are placed opposite one another, so that the two gas streams collide and deflect each other upwards and away from the exhaust port. It is called "loop scavenging."

The piston now begins to travel up the cylinder. First its upper edge covers the transfer ports, thus sealing the crankcase. Almost immediately afterwards it closes the exhaust ports, and the cylinder, too, is sealed. The rising piston now begins to compress the fresh charge trapped in the cylinder.

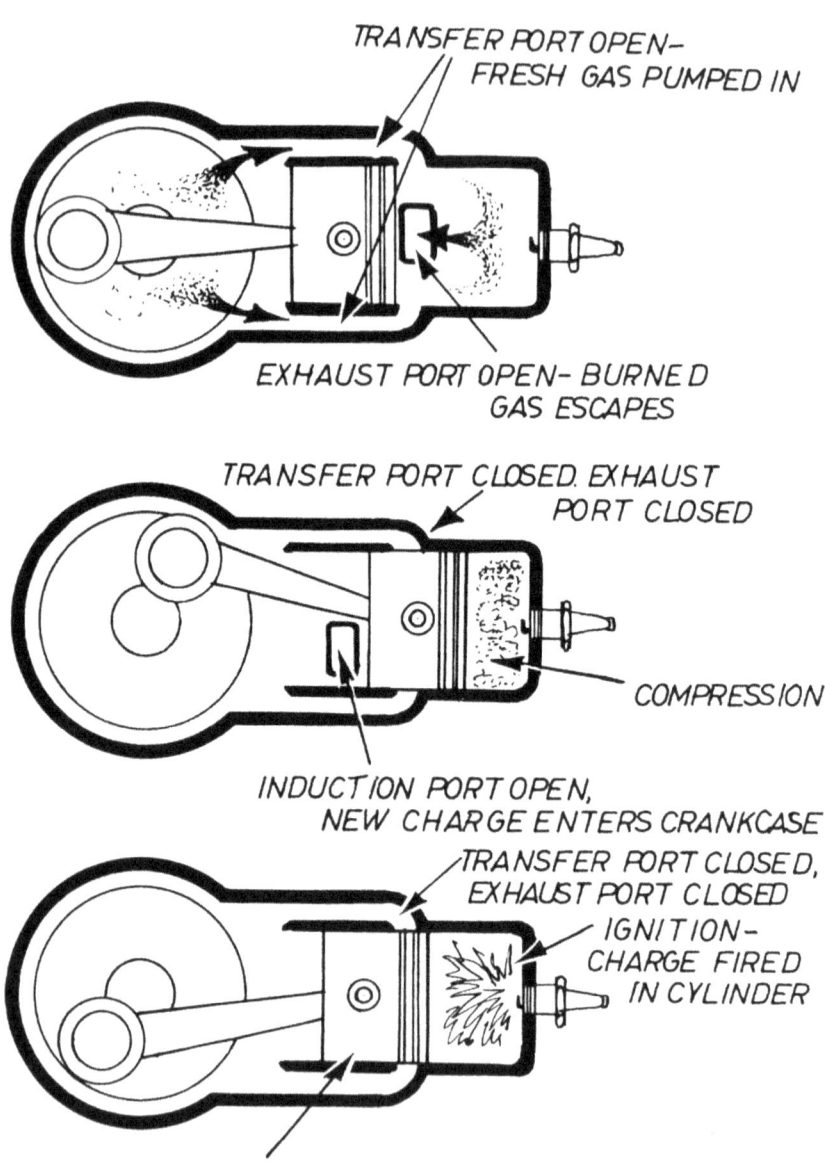

Fig. 1. The Vespa engine in action. How the two-stroke cycle works, in diagrammatic form

BACKGROUND FOR BEGINNERS

As the piston nears TDC its lower edge uncovers the inlet port and a charge is drawn into the crankcase. Just before TDC a spark occurs in the combustion chamber and the mixture ignites. Its expansion thrusts the piston down the cylinder on a power stroke. As it descends it first covers the inlet port, and the under-side of the piston then begins to compress the fresh mixture trapped in the crankcase.

Towards the end of the stroke the top edge of the piston uncovers the exhaust port, through which the burnt gases rush, carried by their own momentum. A split second later the top of the piston uncovers the transfer ports, and the underside of the piston begins to pump the fresh charge out of the crankcase, through the transfer ports, and into the cylinder.

When considering the working cycle of the two-stroke, therefore, it is necessary to take into account not only what is happening in the cylinder, *but also what is taking place simultaneously in the crankcase.* Each downward stroke of the piston is a power stroke in the cylinder and a compression stroke in the crankcase. Each upward stroke of the piston is a compression stroke in the cylinder and an induction stroke in the crankcase.

Since the two-stroke has twice as many power impulses in a given time as the four-stroke, it might be thought that it would develop twice the power from a given size of cylinder. In practice, it usually develops slightly less nominal power than the equivalent four-stroke. One of the reasons is that the cylinder is never completely clear of exhaust gases, and these "dilute" the fresh mixture. Another reason lies in the port timings dictated by the layout of the engine itself. The exhaust port *has* to be opened first, and it follows that as the port is piston-controlled it must therefore close *last*. Consequently, it remains open for a short period when the transfers are closed and the piston is ascending. Inevitably, some of the fresh mixture which has just been induced is expelled through the exhaust port and lost.

One aid to greater efficiency is the rotary-valve induction system used on many Vespa models. This permits a longer induction period, yet does not involve complications.

Where the two-stroke really gains is in pulling power—"torque" is the technical name for it. This is particularly noticeable on hills.

Another great simplification which the layout of the two-stroke engine permits is the use of petroil lubrication. All engines need oil. Not only does it reduce friction, but it also helps to keep the internal surfaces relatively cool.

With a four-stroke, it is necessary to use an independent oiling system, fed by a pump which delivers oil from a sump or oil tank, through passage-ways to bearings, the cylinder walls, and the valve gear. This is, of course, highly efficient—but it calls for the pump itself, its auxiliary drive, its oil container, filters, drain plugs and passages.

The two-stroke, however, has its mixture delivered into the crankcase first. If oil is mixed with this fuel, it means that it can be taken into the

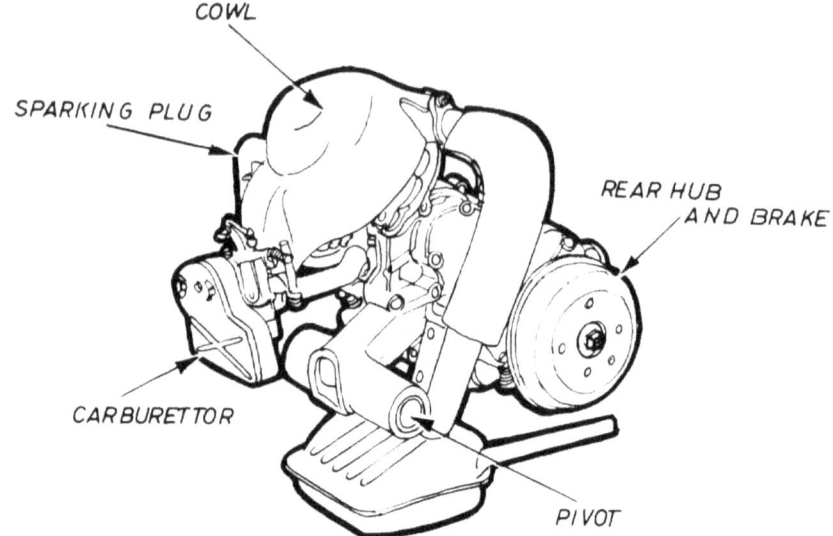

Fig. 2. The Vespa 90 engine/transmission unit. For all major work it is simplest to detach the unit from the frame

case and distributed over the bearings and moving parts without any mechanical complication at all. Furthermore, oily mixture is also fed straight into the cylinder from the crankcase, thus giving continual cylinder-wall oiling—by the incoming mixture on the piston's "cylinder compression" stroke, and by the transfer period at the end of the power stroke.

Crude though it may appear at first glance, the petroil system works well in practice, and it has the added advantage that when climbing hills the engine receives an adequate supply of oil, since the amount induced is proportional to throttle opening and not merely to engine speed. On the other hand, when descending a hill with the throttle closed, the two-stroke can be partially starved of oil, although enough has usually condensed on the crankcase walls to form an inbuilt reserve which offsets this slight disadvantage.

THE CARBURETTOR

We noted, in passing, that when air is induced into the cylinder it is mixed with fuel to form a combustible mixture. This, of course, is a drastic understatement of the magnitude of the job performed by the simple but precision-engineered instrument known as the carburettor (Figs. 11 and 12, pages 38 and 39).

In principle, this is little more than a glorified scent spray. but it has to carry out one of the most crucial of all jobs—metering out a precise and

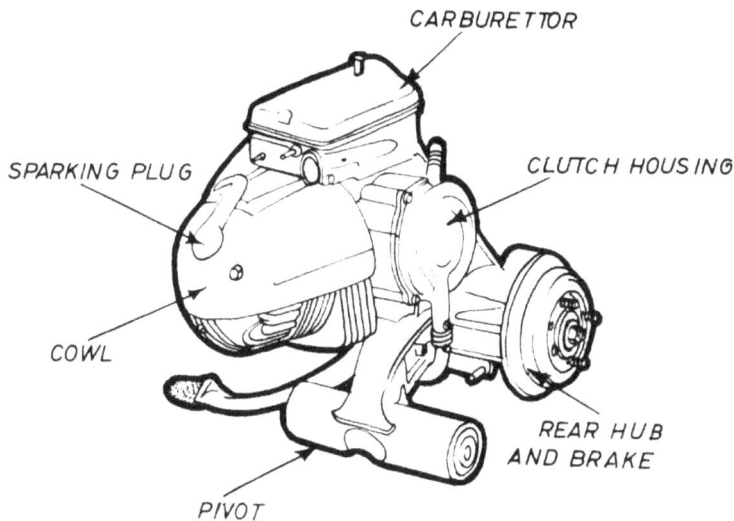

Fig. 3. The Vespa 125/150 engine/transmission unit. As with the smaller models, the unit is easy to remove

minute ration of fuel and mixing it thoroughly with air in just the right proportion to enable it to be burned efficiently.

At first sight, this may not appear to be over-exacting, since the ideal ratio is around 1 part of fuel to 14 parts of air. This, however, is the proportion by *weight;* the carburettor operates by *volume,* and on this basis each 100 c.c of combustible mixture needs to contain only about 0·2 c.c. of fuel, the remaining 99·8 c.c. being air! Obviously, the carburettor despite its simplicity, is a precision instrument and has to be treated accordingly.

The basic components of a carburettor are a float chamber; a venturi (or choke) through which air is drawn; jets, which meter the fuel; and a throttle slide, which controls the amount of mixture which can pass through the carburettor and into the engine.

Consider, first, the basic method of operation. Fuel is fed to the float chamber. This is very much like a pocket edition of the familiar domestic cistern. The chamber contains a float, which rises as fuel is admitted through a valve. In rising, the float carries with it a tapered needle, and this needle is carefully contoured to fit in a seat in the valve. When the level inside the chamber is correct, the needle is pressed fully home on its seating, thus cutting off the flow of fuel. When the level in the chamber falls the float falls with it, and so does the needle. Leaving its seating, it permits more fuel to flow into the chamber, until the correct level is again reached.

Immersed in the float chamber is a tube, the upper end of which opens into the venturi. Screwed to the bottom of this tube is a jet—an essential part of the carburettor which looks suspiciously like a small screw or bolt with a hole drilled through the centre. That, in fact, is just what it is—but the hole is so proportioned that it will pass just the right amount of fuel and no more. When the crankcase induction stroke begins, air is drawn through the carburettor venturi, which is so shaped that there is a fall in pressure in the section—called the mixing chamber—around the jet tube. As a result, fuel is drawn up the tube into the chamber, where it mixes with the air before passing through the inlet port into the crankcase.

Obviously, a carburettor which consisted of these parts alone would work, but the engine would run at only one speed. Some means of varying the supply of mixture has to be arranged, and this means has to be one which keeps the essential fuel-air proportion at all openings. The answer is to use a throttle slide to vary the amount of air admitted.

This is how such a system works. A cable, connected to the throttle control, pulls the slide upwards, and a light spring returns it when the control is slackened.

When the throttle is closed only a very small amount of air can pass under the slide—so small, in fact, that it is impossible for the main jet to meter out the tiny amount of fuel required. For running under these conditions a very fine slow-running jet delivers a minute ration of fuel to the mixing chamber.

As the throttle is opened, the slide is raised. More air passes through the venturi, drawing more fuel through the main jet. Further movement of the throttle increases both the amount of air permitted to pass and the amount of fuel which the jet supplies, until at full throttle both passages are supplying the maximum amounts of which they are capable.

Since the proper action of the carburettor depends upon the operation of very fine metering devices, great attention must be paid to ensuring that the internals are kept free of dirt. Even a speck of dirt is quite enough to block the jet and thus prevent fuel passing through it. The petroil is, therefore, normally filtered at several points by passing through fine wire mesh. One such filter is usually fitted round the inlet of the on/off tap, in the fuel tank, and a second filter protects the needle valve.

When an engine is cold it needs a somewhat richer mixture than usual to enable it to start, and to supply this it is usual to employ a starter unit, which richens the mixture without cutting the air supply.

All Vespa carburettors, besides being equipped with fuel filters, also have a filter for the air. This is not so much to protect the carburettor as to protect the engine, since the air usually contains dust; and dust, harmless though it may look, contains a surprising number of very hard particles which are quite capable of scratching the working parts of the engine very badly indeed.

An air filter itself forms an obstacle to the air flow and cuts the amount of air entering the carburettor. In the design stage, this obstruction is taken into consideration and the fuel is metered accordingly. If, therefore, an instrument which is intended to have an air filter is used without one, the effect is to weaken the resulting mixture, since more air is entering while the fuel supply remains unaltered. Damage to the internal parts of the engine apart, this is one reason why the engine should not be run with the air filter removed.

THE IGNITION SYSTEM

Even really experienced riders often have only the slightest knowledge of the working of the electrical system upon which the whole operation of the engine depends. As a result, the electrics are frequently neglected, failure results—and the immediate conclusion is that electricity is thoroughly unreliable anyway! There is no need, however, to be a qualified electrical engineer to understand *how* the system works.

All electrical practice is founded upon circuits, and upon the fact that an electric current will invariably take the shortest path to earth. In this connection, though, it should be emphasized that "earth" does not necessarily mean the ground. As far as a scooter's electrical system is concerned, "earth" is the mass of the scooter itself, a little world all of its own.

A circuit is just what its name implies. In this, electricity is rather like a model railway. If all the points are correctly set, the train will go round and round. If they are not, it will simply end up standing still.

As with the train, so with electricity. Provided there is a circuit, the current will flow. If the circuit is broken, it will not. And just occasionally there may be some points badly set which direct it straight to earth—a short-circuit; just as if the train had been directed on to a branch line leading straight to a siding.

Electricity is measured in volts and amperes. The volt is a measure of its force: the ampere basically a measure of the number of electrons per second passing a given point within the electrical circuit. In other words, while voltage indicates the electrical pressure in the circuit, amperes indicate the quantity of electricity which is flowing. The resistance to the flow presented by the wires and so forth which make up the circuit is measured in ohms, one ohm being a resistance which calls for one volt to be applied so that one ampere may flow.

Electricity is further regarded as comprising two basic types of current—positive and negative—but for all practical purposes it is only necessary to know that these do, in fact, exist. Finally it is necessary to accept one further basic fact: that when a coil is placed in a magnetic field electricity is produced.

Two types of machine for producing electricity are used on engines—the a.c. generator and the d.c. generator. The first produces an alternating current—one which has a constantly reversing flow. The second produces direct current, which flows in one direction only. On Vespas a d.c. flywheel magneto-generator is employed (Figs. 15 and 16, pages 45 and 46).

In this design permanent magnets are mounted inside the rim of the external flywheel, and a stator plate (bolted to the engine) holds an ignition coil and lighting coils, each being closely-wound coils of fine wire. They are different, however, in that the ignition coil is really two coils in one—a low-tension primary winding surrounding a high-tension secondary winding, but insulated from it. Sometimes this high-tension coil is mounted externally and current is fed from low-tension coils on the stator plate.

There is one other essential part—the contact-breaker. This is simply a mechanical switch, consisting of a pair of points which are opened and closed by a cam carried on the engine mainshaft. Electrically, the contact-breaker is connected into the low-tension side of the ignition circuit.

From the high-tension winding of the ignition coil, a heavily insulated high-tension lead is connected to the sparking plug set in the cylinder head. This plug consists of a body and an insulated central electrode to which the high-tension lead is connected. Welded to the body is a side electrode which is set so that a gap of around 20 thousandths of an inch exists between its tip and that of the central electrode.

When the flywheel is revolved, the magnets set up a magnetic field and low-tension electricity is generated in the primary windings of the ignition coil. At a predetermined point, however, the cam presses one of the points of the contact-breaker away from the other and so breaks the circuit.

Here something happens which has to be taken on trust. This sudden rupturing of the low-tension circuit in the primary windings of the ignition coil creates a high-tension current in the coil's secondary windings. This current is of a very high voltage—about 16,000 volts. Seeking the shortest path to earth, it streaks down the high-tension lead. Normally it would stop dead at the gap in the sparking plug, but the pressure behind it is too great to permit it to do so. Instead, it jumps across the gap in the form of a hot blue spark—and it is this spark which ignites the mixture in the cylinder. In a normal scooter two-stroke engine this operation can occur over 5,000 times every minute.

To prevent the low-tension current from doing at the contact-breaker points just what the high-tension current subsequently does at the sparking-plug gap—jumping across in the form of a spark—a small electrical "shock-absorber" called a condenser is added to the circuit.

The lighting systems and horn can be supplied with electricity from a battery, which is charged by current delivered from the L.T. coils, or this current can be taken direct from the coils to the components concerned, which will then operate only when the engine is running.

THE TRANSMISSION

Internal-combustion motors are high-speed engines in which power output is, within limits, proportional to the speed of rotation of the engine. At low speeds, therefore, less power is developed than at high speeds. Where outside factors—such as a hill—increase the load on an engine its

BACKGROUND FOR BEGINNERS

speed, and consequently its power, falls off. This, in turn, reduces its speed still more, causing a further drop in power. At length, the load becomes so great that it overcomes the remaining power of the engine and the motor "stalls."

Basically, there is a comparatively narrow range of engine speed at which the greatest power is developed and the engine should, ideally, run at this speed whenever possible. The designer does in fact try to arrange for this to coincide with the top-gear cruising speed. To deal with varying loads, however, some means of keeping engine speed high when road speed falls is necessary, and this need is met by the gearbox (Fig. 6, page 31).

This consists basically of *input* and *output* shafts, on which are carried a series of meshing gears. Each pair of gears gives a different reduction between the speeds of the two shafts. Only one pair of gears can be used to transmit the power at any one time.

Initially, the primary drive (Figs. 7 and 8, pages 32 and 33) which transmits the crankshaft movement to the gearbox provides the first reduction in speed, cutting the rotational speed by approximately one half. This is reduced still further in the gearbox itself, depending upon which pair of gears is locked into position on the shafts. In top gear, therefore, the engine crankshaft may revolve six times for each revolution of the rear wheel, but in bottom gear it will turn over seventeen times. In one revolution of the rear wheel, then, top gear allows the power of six power strokes to be applied. But in bottom gear—in the same distance covered— the power of seventeen strokes is passed through to the driving wheel. Thus an increase in load can be counterbalanced by changing into a lower gear, bringing more power to bear in a given distance at the cost of a drop in road speed.

The method employed to lock the various gears to the shafts is supremely simple. On the input shaft all gears revolve with the shaft; on the output shaft all the gears run free, but are constantly meshed with the input gears. Each free-running gear in turn can be locked to the shaft when a sliding member is moved sideways by a selector, whose movement is dictated by a twist grip and cable control.

A vital part of the transmission is the clutch, which enables the drive to be freed at will (Fig. 12, page 39). A clutch consists of one member driven by the engine, a second member which is connected to the transmission, and friction plates which link the two, together with springs and a withdrawal mechanism. There is thus no direct connection between the engine and the transmission. All the drive is taken through the clutch plates.

The clutch has two main parts: the clutch centre and the clutch body. The clutch centre has a series of splines on its boss, and the clutch body a series of splines round its inner periphery. Inside, a pressure plate and a series of clutch plates are fitted. Half these carry friction linings. Alternate plates are splined round the outer edge to match the splining of the clutch body. Strong springs, held by a spring plate, press all these plates hard together.

When the clutch is driven by the crankshaft it turns and, owing to the pressure exerted by the springs, the friction between the plates is such that they also turn as one unit and in so doing transmit the drive. When the withdrawal mechanism is operated the pressure of the springs is relieved. The part of the clutch driven from the engine—and the plates fixed to it—still revolve, but the friction between these and the remaining plates is now too low to transmit movement. The lined plates therefore remain stationary, and so does that part of the clutch fixed to the primary drive. Thus no power is transmitted.

By gradually releasing the withdrawal mechanism, the revolving plates can be brought into increasing contact with the stationary plates. At first, these "slip"; but as contact is increased they speed up, until with the full spring pressure restored the whole clutch is once again rotating as a complete unit. This is what happens each time a scooter moves off from a standstill.

RUNNING GEAR

When a scooter is driven along a road it remains upright for exactly the same reason that a gyroscope refuses to topple over; the two revolving wheels do, in effect, act as a pair of gyroscopes and resist all attempts to force them out of their course.

There are, however, other factors which enter into it. One is the design of the steering. This is so arranged that the front wheel is trailing rather like the castor of an armchair. The characteristics of the steering depend to some extent upon the amount of "trail" specified by the designer, and to some extent upon other factors. One of these is the "rake"—the angle at which the steering head is set—and others are the weight distribution of the machine as a whole and the position of its centre of gravity.

In addition, the manner in which the suspension systems act plays a great part in determining whether the scooter handles well or not. The Vespa design utilizes a trailing link front fork, in which a short arm carrying the wheel moves upwards and backwards against the resistance of a spring (Figs. 24–6, pages 57–9). This movement has to be damped. If there were no damper, the spring would thrust the wheel up and down with a rapid action, and so cause the front end of the machine to pitch up and down. That's just what did happen on very early models.

To prevent this, a hydraulic damper is used. It consists of an oil chamber and a disc valve, so designed that when the sliding member rises it permits the oil to pass through with little or no resistance. On the return stroke the valve is partially closed, and this slows down the rate at which the oil can return to the chamber, causing considerable friction through oil drag. In consequence, the return stroke of the trailing link is also slowed down, thereby preventing spring oscillation. A similar layout is adopted at the rear, where the suspension is controlled by a large coil spring and an independent hydraulic damper.

BACKGROUND FOR BEGINNERS 13

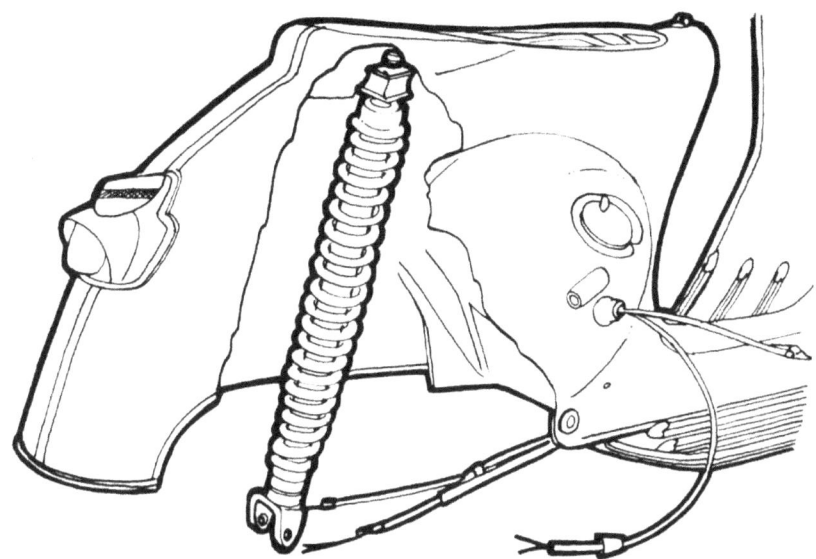

Fig. 4. Under the body. The control cables and electrics have been disconnected, the rear suspension fastening undone, and the pivot bolt removed. This is all that is required to detach the engine unit

Just as important as making the scooter move is the ability to make it stop. This is the job of the brakes, which are of the internal-expanding type. Each wheel carries a drum, the inside surfaces of which are accurately ground so that the drum is completely round and true.

Closing the drum is a back-plate, and affixed to this plate is a pivot pin. Diametrically opposed to the pin is a cam, which is connected to the brake lever. Two brake shoes—semi-circular in shape, with a friction lining riveted to the outer curve on each—are fitted with one end butting on the pivot pin and the other on one face of the cam. They are held together by a spring and the whole back-plate assembly is fixed rigidly to the machine.

When the brake lever or pedal is operated, the cam turns and presses the free ends of the shoes outwards. This brings the friction linings into contact with the inside surface of the drum, decelerating the machine.

A brake is basically a form of heat-exchanger. The friction created by the linings rubbing on the surface of the drum absorbs energy which would otherwise be devoted to driving the scooter, and this energy is converted into heat, which is dissipated from the surface of the drum.

Both brakes on Vespas are controlled by cables. In addition, cables are used for the throttle, clutch and gear controls. For efficient operation, a cable depends upon the correct relationship between its inner and outer wires being maintained. Since the inner wires have tendency to stretch, the outer casings are provided with screwed adjusters which enable the effective length of the outer casing to be varied in relation to the inner wire. All cables work either against the resistance of a spring, by which the return action is supplied, or against the pull of a second cable operating in an opposite direction, since cables normally perform well only when used in tension.

3 Don't forget your tools

WHEN the plumber forgets his tools it's a joke. But it's not so funny if you forget to provide yourself with a decent tool kit before you set out to maintain or overhaul a scooter. You just can't do the job with inadequate tools. To carry out even routine maintenance properly calls for the use of a good set of spanners, while major overhauls—which at the factory quite often require the use of special tools—demand a top-quality tool kit.

It's no use relying on the standard tool roll. That is designed to cope only with roadside emergencies and to carry out some of the easier routine jobs. It is *not* intended for the stern work of stripping the engine unit! So, having spent well over a hundred pounds to get yourself a first-class scooter, lash out a fiver or so more on a tool kit to match. Cheap tools are almost invariably a bad investment. They do not wear well, and they also have an infuriating habit of ruining nuts and bolts.

The first essential is to buy a really good set of chrome-vanadium open-ended spanners in metric sizes. A set of half a dozen spanners will give a range of sizes sufficient for most work and will cost, at worst, a couple of pounds.

Next, it is vital to have a set of strong metric box spanners—or, better still, socket spanners. Ring spanners are more of a luxury. They are less handy in confined spaces than are open-enders or sockets, although they do give a very good grip. In addition, you will need a pair of really good screwdrivers, with insulated handles. One screwdriver with a 5/16 in. blade and an electrical screwdriver with a long 1/8 in. blade are the minimum requirements. And don't forget two pairs of pliers—one of them the insulated-handled long-nose type. They are indispensable for electrical work and for use on the control cables.

You'll need a couple of hammers, one of them with soft faces, and a drift or two. Feeler gauges are essential, and a plug gapping tool is handy. And carry your own tyre pressure gauge, for garage air-line gauges are highly suspect.

There is far more to using even the simplest of hand tools than merely placing them in position and tugging hard. Each particular type of spanner has its own characteristics, and each is better suited to one particular type of job. The factory places great stress on using the right tools for every operation.

Open-ended spanners are the great all-rounders of the kit. They can be used in confined spaces and they have the advantage that the jaws are angled, so that reversing the spanner will give fresh "purchase" on the nut. This is most useful when the nut in question is somewhat inaccessible, since it can be freed in stages simply by constantly reversing the spanner.

It is, of course, essential that only the right size of spanner should be used. The open-ender applies its pressure on the flats of the nut or bolt, and is consequently made with jaws of just the right width to grip them. If too large a spanner is used the jaws will press against the angles of the bolt instead of the flats. One or two things then happens: either the spanner gouges away the metal of the head, leaving a rounded surface which no spanner on earth could ever again grip, or else the bolt head slightly springs the jaws of the spanner itself, which is promptly ruined. Or, of course, you can get the worst of both worlds and ruin both bolt and spanner together!

Damage to the jaws can also be caused by applying excessive force when trying to free a bolt which refuses to budge. There is a temptation, in these circumstances, to slip a piece of piping over the free end of the spanner to increase the leverage. This is permissible in an emergency, provided due care is used, but if you are none too experienced as a mechanic it is inadvisable to try it. You are more likely to spring the spanner's jaws or snap the bolt. Douse the bolt with penetrating oil and await results—or use a socket spanner instead. Socket, box, or ring spanners are at a great advantage when it comes to shifting recalcitrant nuts. Rings and sockets both grip on the angles, not the flats, of the bolt and consequently apply pressure at half a dozen points where the open-ended spanner can do so only on two surfaces.

If a nut or bolt is really obstinate, try heating it with a small gas torch or flood it with penetrating-oil or paraffin and leave it overnight. You'll save time in the long run compared with the tedious job of drilling out a fractured bolt or stud. If you *have* a gas torch, though, a gentle application of local heat will often give results in a few minutes.

A box spanner can apply its force on both angles and flats provided it fits well (cheap box spanners rarely do) but frequently the weak point here is the tommy bar used to turn the box, which simply bends under the strain. Another drawback with box spanners is that, owing to the offset between the part of the spanner which holds the nut and the holes through which the tommy bar passes, the spanner may tend to ride off the hexagon when pressure is applied.

When using a spanner to tighten nuts or bolts it is important to remember that too much force should not be used. Strong hand pressure is sufficient to lock the size of nut or bolt for which the spanner is intended. If excessive force is used, the actual material of the bolt can be weakened sufficiently to cause a fracture. This should be borne particularly in mind when tightening bolts which are threaded into light alloy. Here, the steel bolt is much harder than the material forming the internal threads, and overenthusiasm with the spanner can easily strip the thread in the hole. The only real solution, then, is to drill out the hole and re-tap it to take a larger-sized bolt.

Pliers, of course, should never be used as makeshift spanners, since the jaws can never be parallel and the serrated pipe grip is almost perilously liable to slip. A rounded hexagon is the inevitable result if it does. If you do need to lock on to a hexagon use a mole-type wrench. It will damage it—but at least it will grip it firmly.

Adjustable spanners should never be allowed near the machine. They are a butcher's tool, not a mechanic's. True, an "adjustable" can be useful in an emergency—but for workshop maintenance it is best forgotten since, again, the jaws can never be aligned accurately enough to obviate the danger of slipping.

Screwdrivers should have their blades properly ground so that, in side view, the blade is at first concave, and then runs parallel all the way to the tip. This enables it to be seated properly in the slot and to apply its pressure evenly. A screwdriver whose blade is wedge-shaped when viewed from the side cannot seat properly and exerts all its force on the upper edges of the slot. Understandably, these crumble under the strain and the screw is useless thereafter.

After use, all tools should be wiped clean, kept in a dry place, and protected from dust by being wrapped in rag. If they are used fairly infrequently they should also be very lightly oiled. The film of lubrication should, of course, be wiped off before they are used again.

4 Put method in your maintenance

You wouldn't want a heart transplant whenever you caught a chill—and neither does your scooter. There's a world of difference between routine maintenance—the day-to-day adjustments and minor repairs which all vehicles need—and major overhauls. Both have their place in keeping a scooter in good working order, but while the machine will repay you for punctilious attention to its everyday needs it will not run properly and give of its best if the engine is never allowed to settle down. So far as major work is concerned, the best course is to leave a component alone so long as it is working well.

If the routine maintenance is neglected it's a different story. The time which can elapse between overhauls is drastically shortened and the amount of work needing to be done (and the amount of money needing to be spent) will be painfully increased.

The reason for this is simple enough. Maladjustments have a cumulative effect. Little enough harm, for example, will result if a sparking plug is loose and the scooter covers 20 miles or so before the fault is discovered. But if, in the absence of a routine check, the loose plug is left for a thousand miles the results can be serious. All sorts of troubles could spring from this one minor example of neglect. Hot gases could burn away the lower threads in the plug hole, and the wobbling plug could elongate the hole itself. The compression would be reduced, so the engine could never develop its full power. Result? Less performance and a high fuel consumption.

Worse still, extra air drawn in through the plug hole would give a weak mixture, causing overheating and possible distortion of the barrel and piston. Seizure might result. At the very least, a new head could be required —and you might easily find yourself paying for a barrel and piston as well. A pretty stiff price, that, for the minute saved by omitting to make a single, simple check.

Or consider the brakes, and that gradual deterioration I mentioned earlier. Unless their power and adjustment is constantly checked you may easily find that when an emergency stop has to be made in a distance of forty feet the scooter will not stop in less than forty-five. The result can be very expensive indeed—and it's a dangerous way of learning a lesson.

Constant and methodical inspection is the best way of preventing troubles. The usual recommendations are based on elapsed mileage, but in practice these are difficult to carry out if a full log of the work already done is not kept.

This was a problem which faced the armed forces, and to combat it the military authorities evolved task systems which called for a daily or weekly check on each aspect of the mechanical side of the vehicle.

Nowadays the Automobile Association uses a similar idea for maintaining its patrol vans—and when did you last see one of those at the wrong end of a tow-rope? The AA Minivans cover upwards of 100,000 miles on one top overhaul: and the reason is conscientious routine maintenance.

In a modified form, "task" systems are ideally suited for your scooter. They can be of two types, daily or weekly. Which is employed depends entirely on the use to which the scooter is put. If it is a "ride-to-work" machine, checks should be made each day. If it is employed solely for weekend excursions, a weekly basis can be substituted.

Taking the daily system first, here is a maintenance check routine for Vespas. Though it covers all the major parts which need to be checked, to carry out these recommendations should never involve the expenditure of more than ten minutes in a single day. In most cases only a couple of minutes will be needed.

DAILY SYSTEMS

Sunday: check the adjustment of front and rear brakes; check freedom of action of brake controls; check security of nuts and bolts in braking system; check lubrication of brake cables.

Monday: check gearbox oil level; check all controls for free movement and adequate lubrication.

Tuesday: check sparking plug for gap and condition; check battery.

Wednesday: examine tyre treads, check for depth, and remove any trapped stones; check tyre pressures; check wheels for security; rock wheels and front fork to check play in bearings.

Thursday: check clutch cable for adjustment; check that clutch plates are freeing.

Friday: check all nuts and bolts for security; check petrol flow.

Saturday: check all exposed electrical wiring for signs of abrasion or fracture; check all electrical terminals for tightness; check operation of horn, lamps and dip-switch; check contact-breaker settings.

ALTERNATIVE WEEKLY SYSTEMS

Week 1: check gearbox oil level; check plug for gap and condition.

Week 2: check brakes for adjustment, freedom and control action, and lubrication of cables; check wheels for security; rock wheels and front fork to check play in bearings; examine tyre treads and adjust pressures.

Week 3: examine all electrical leads for signs of abrasion or fracture;

check all terminals for security; check operation of horn, lamps and dip-switch; check contact-breaker setting; check battery.

Week 4: check clutch cable for adjustment; check that clutch plates are freeing; check all nuts and bolts for security.

By employing the daily system you can ensure that most of the major points are checked at least once each week. Even allowing for a pretty substantial mileage each day this should mean, at the worst, that no fault could go undetected for more than, say, 300 miles. So most defects would be discovered well before they had time to develop to serious proportions.

With the weekly system, a month could elapse between the beginning of a fault and its discovery. Where the machine is used for only a 50-mile week-end jaunt this would be neither here nor there—but if the machine is used more frequently than this it's best to settle for the daily checks instead.

The important thing is to *check* the relevant points. In nine cases out of ten no adjustment will be necessary: you are only examining the component to find out if it needs to be touched, and where everything is in order you merely leave well alone and pass on to the next point on the list.

Neither system, however, takes into account periodic oil changing and greasing, which must still be carried out on the elapsed mileage basis recommended by the manufacturer. As it's all too easy to forget just when the job was last done, a useful aid to memory in this department is to stick a piece of self-adhesive tape to the parts concerned, noting on the tape the mileage at which the work was last done, or the mileage at which it should next be done.

A word of warning, here, about grades of oil and greases. The Appendix lists certain grades of lubricant which should be used. The manufacturers do not pick these names out of a hat; nor do they suggest them because they get a "rake-off" from the oil companies. They don't!

The factory and the research departments of the oil companies both carry out long and expensive tests with the various components, using a wide range of oils and greases. The brands which give the best results—longest life with the least friction—are the brands which are eventually recommended. So stick to them and do not be tempted to use a different grade of lubricant because it is cheaper or because you have read in an advertisement that it has some magical properties. It may well have them, but unless they happen to be the right properties for your particular machine the results may not be as pleasant as you think. Multigrade oils, in particular, are not suitable for two-stroke engines and must never be used. Stick to the specially compounded two-stroke oils that have been devised to suit your engine.

5 Be your own doctor

TELL your doctor that you're ill and he will make a diagnosis by methodically listing your symptoms to build up an overall picture of the complaint. This done, he can identify it and treat you accordingly.

When your scooter's sick, you are the doctor—and it's up to you to make the same type of diagnosis from the symptoms you observe. Obviously there is a fault—some reason *why* the engine will not work—and before it can be cured it must first be located and identified.

Now, there's one basic starting point. If certain minimum requirements are being fulfilled then the engine *must* work. If it is not working, then it follows that at least one of these requirements is not being met, and fault tracing boils down to discovering which it is, and why it is not being supplied.

An engine *must* work if the correct charge of fuel-air mixture is being induced into the crankcase, transferred to the cylinder, properly compressed, fired at the right moment, and the residue properly exhausted. Only an obvious mechanical failure could then stop the unit.

Consequently fault tracing should always begin with an investigation into these five main requirements, and logically it must start with checking the petroil supply by peering into the tank to see that, in fact, there is a supply of fuel available. The next step should then be the equally obvious one of checking that the fuel is turned on and, if the tank level is low, that the tap is turned to the reserve position.

Once assured that the tank does contain fuel and that the tap is correctly set, the next check on the list is to ascertain whether or not the fuel is reaching the carburettor. It could be prevented by a blockage in the tap, by a blockage in the pipe, by an air lock, by a choked filter, or by a jammed needle valve.

Normally, this initial check will have taken only a minute or so to carry out, but it will have given one of two quite definite answers. Either fuel is reaching the carburettor, or it is not. If it is not, then you have found at least a contributory cause of the trouble, and this should be rectified before proceeding. If it is reaching the carburettor, you can pass on to the next stage which, with a two-stroke, must always be to check the sparking plug, especially if carburettor flooding has occurred.

Where the engine has been badly overflooded, neat fuel will be trapped in the crankcase, and there will be no chance of starting. Take out the plug, drain all fuel from the float chamber, and switch off the petrol. Then open the throttle wide, so that you admit as much air as possible, and turn the unit on the kick-starter, briskly, about a dozen times. This should eject most of the trapped fuel. If the plug is wet, dry it. If necessary, burn the petrol off by holding the plug in the flame of a cigarette lighter or a match. Then check the gap and replace it. Connect the h.t. lead and operate the kick-starter. If the engine then fires, turn on the fuel. If it does not, turn on the fuel, allow a few seconds for the float chamber to fill, and then kick it again. It should then work satisfactorily.

If the initial inspection of the fuel system has brought no obvious fault to light, the next stage of the fault tracing should be switched to the ignition system. This is always a strong suspect with two-strokes, which tend to be very touchy indeed about their sparking plugs. So, first of all, remove the plug and clean it with a hard-bristled brush—not a wire brush, that can deposit metal traces on the insulator and make matters worse—and regap it before replacing it.

Persistent plug trouble can indicate that the wrong grade of plug is fitted, or that the engine is running too hot. This, in turn, points to poor scavenging or a weak mixture, and should suggest that either the exhaust system is becoming choked, or that a joint is leaking.

Where inspection of the plug shows the spark gap to be correct and the business parts (including the insulator) clean, connect the plug to the h.t. lead and place its metal body in contact with the cylinder. Arrange matters so that you can easily see the gap while operating the kick-starter, and then turn the motor over smartly. A good fat spark should jump across the plug points. Repeat the check several times, and if no spark is obtained substitute a brand-new plug—an essential "spare" which should always be carried—and try again. If the new plug sparks and the old one didn't, the obvious inference is that the plug insulation has broken down, and fitting the new plug in its place should cure the trouble.

If no spark is obtained with the new plug, however, then the trouble lies somewhere between the sparking-plug terminal and the magneto, and a more exhaustive examination will have to be made.

Examine the h.t. lead minutely throughout its length, checking the terminals and inspecting the insulation for signs of cracks or perished areas which could be leading to a short-circuit. If you are doubtful about it, try the effect of substituting a spare length of h.t. lead and retesting with that. Examine all the electrical connections on the h.t. and l.t. side of the machine with an external coil.

Finally, remove the inspection plate on the flywheel and take a look at the contact-breaker points. Open them fully and see if they are worn or dirty. Clean them by inserting a clean slip of card, close the points lightly on it, and withdraw it against their pressure. Do this two or three times, until the card comes away clean and dry. Then open the points fully again and check the gap with a feeler gauge. If everything seems to be in order you have then done all that is possible on the electrical side, so far as roadside checking is concerned. A full ignition test is a garage job.

Complete engine failure for any other cause is unlikely, except in the event of the piston rings being broken following a seizure. Other troubles are more likely to show themselves in reduced performance or in erratic running.

One of the likelier causes of a lack of pulling power, for instance, is loss of compression and it is possible, where this is suspected, to deduce where the fault lies from the way the engine behaves. If the crankcase seals have failed there will be a tendency for the unit to split back through the carburettor, since extra air will be induced into the crankcase, thus weakening the mixture. Where the head joint is fractured, a characteristic hissing noise may be heard as gas is driven through the gap. In both cases the unit will tend to run hot and this, in turn, aggravates the trouble.

Following a seizure, as we have noted, the rings may have fractured. Or, on an engine which has not been decarbonized regularly, the rings may have "gummed up" in their grooves. This not only reduces both crankcase and cylinder compressions but it also allows oil to be driven from the case into the cylinder. This oil burns, and the resulting smoke issuing from the tail pipe is a good clue to watch for. If at any time you have partially seized your engine, and immediately afterwards it loses performance and begins to smoke, the only wise course is to stop immediately. The rings have almost certainly been damaged, and any further running could seriously damage the bore too. This is especially the case where a ring has broken, for its sharp edges will act as highly efficient cutting tools, and the cylinder can be ruined.

One puzzling fault is pre-ignition. The engine "pinks" continually—a metallic tinkling sound—and will even continue to run when the ignition is cut. This is caused by carbon deposits or a small sliver of metal in the head becoming red hot and igniting the mixture before the spark occurs. The cure is to decarbonize as soon as you possibly can.

Exactly the same process of elimination has to be followed when tracing faults in the lighting system. Faced with electricity, of course, most laymen simply give it best first time, but in fact electrical work is reasonably straightforward provided that magic word "circuit" is borne in mind. Circuits are the key to electricity. If electricity is present and the circuit is complete then the current *must* flow through it. If electricity is present but is not flowing then it follows that the circuit is not complete.

Faulty circuits are of two types—the open circuit and the short-circuit. In the first case there is a complete break and the wires on the side of the breakage remote from the electrical source are "dead." In the case of a short-circuit the current is still flowing, but it is following a shorter path to earth, as would happen, for instance, if one end of a live lead had become detached from its terminal and had earthed itself on the bodywork.

Obviously, then, the first stage is to find out which wire is affected, and to do this it is necessary to be able to read a wiring diagram. Such a diagram may, at first sight, appear disconcertingly like a plan of a railway marshalling yard—and, oddly enough, it is not all a bad idea to think of it as such. The leads become railway lines, and the current the train which has to pass over them. Remember, though, that one important main line is not shown. This is the earth return, formed by the actual framework of the scooter itself. All the components are connected to this earth, which, therefore, forms one complete half of the circuit.

Where really complicated circuits are involved, it sometimes helps to trace them out individually, placing tracing paper over the wiring diagram and following the various lines until you have a picture of the complete circuit, with all its intermediate "stations" marked.

Having found the circuit, the next job is to check it. First, obviously, you have to discover whether any current is flowing or not—on direct-lighting models, of course, the engine must be running—and here a test rig helps immensely. One can be made quite simply with a bulb, a bulb-holder, and a length of electrical lead.

On models with batteries, first place the bulb-holder against one battery terminal and then touch the other terminal with the end of the lead. The bulb should light. If not, it shows that the battery is flat, and it will have to be recharged before you can proceed. Never forget that a flat battery is more likely to be a symptom of the trouble than the cause. There is almost certainly a short-circuit somewhere, which has caused the battery to drain itself. It is possible for this to be a short-circuit inside the battery itself, so get the garage to check the condition at the same time.

Once you are certain that the battery is all right you must check each individual lead in the circuit in question, a job made considerably easier by the fact that modern wiring harnesses use wires of distinctive colours for each of the individual circuits. Remember, though, that on the Vespa the battery *must* be disconnected whenever you intend to work on the lighting switch.

So, in the case of, say, the circuit to the tail lamp, you would (having checked first the bulb and then the battery) have disconnected it temporarily while the lighting switch was opened up. The end of the lead would then be freed from its terminal, brought clear, and the battery reconnected. The test rig would then have been applied to the open end of the lead; the holder placed against the lead; and the holder wire connected to earth. If the lamp then lit, it would show that current was reaching the terminal. Disconnect the battery again, replace the lead you had removed, and remove the end of the tail-lamp lead from the switch. In its place connect the test-rig lead, and earth the holder. Connect the battery and operate the switch. If it lights the bulb the switch has a clean bill of health, and the fault must lie either in the tail-lamp lead or in the lamp itself.

Continue checking, stage by stage, throughout the entire circuit. You may find, for example, that when the test-rig is connected to the lamp end of the terminal it will not light the bulb. This shows that the fault lies in the lead itself. It has probably fractured, so it must be traced and inspected minutely. If it is a simple fracture you will find two loose ends. Sometimes a short-circuit can be detected by switching on and shaking the machine. As the broken end earths itself a characteristic crackling of electricity can be heard.

More difficult to locate is an internal fracture, where the insulation is undamaged. Garage men use a test rig fitted with a needle-sharp probe which can be pushed through the insulation at various points until a stage is reached at which the test bulb fails to light. This can literally pin-point the position of the breakage. An alternative is to pull two ways on the lead, at intervals of about three inches, until a section is found which stretches under such treatment. This is the section in which the break has occurred.

Where the suspect lead is a very long one, or is inaccessible, a double check and a temporary repair can be made by connecting the two terminals with an external length of wire. Sometimes a new lead can be drawn through the conduit by wiring it to the old lead and pulling it through with it.

When repairing fractured leads it is important to ensure that no undue electrical stresses are set up and that the insulation is made good. All joints should be twisted together as neatly as possible—it is even better if they can be soldered—and the new joint must be wound round with insulating tape to make leakage impossible. Any terminals which have been undone must be refitted tightly, and if a soldered joint has failed it *must* be resoldered. It is not sufficient to tape it up.

Given patience and a modicum of equipment, there is no reason why you should not be able to trace most faults which can occur either in the engine or in the electrical system. Even when the nature of the failure is such that it is not possible to repair it oneself, it is often possible to provide a temporary cure, or at least to save money by giving the repairer an accurate diagnosis of the trouble.

TROUBLE TRACING

Here is the factory's own basic trouble-tracing sequence, recommended for work in the garage. For ready reference, there's a simplified trouble-tracing chart in Appendix 2 that will help you to diagnose troubles that occur on the road too.

Starting Difficulties

Check the sparking plug. If it is not sparking, or if the spark is weak or irregular, then the following possibilities should be investigated:

1 Wrong grade of plug.
2 Plug gap incorrect.
3 Plug dirty or wet.
4 Plug "cooked."
5 Plug cap tracking.

6 H.t. lead faulty.
7 Battery discharged or badly connected.
8 Rectifier faulty.
9 Contact-breaker points dirty, wet, or incorrectly gapped.
10 Ignition timing wrongly set.
11 Condenser faulty.
12 Coil faulty.

If the plug is sparking, check:

1 Is the choke opening properly?
2 Is the engine flooded?
3 Is the carburettor float valve operating properly?
4 Are you starting without choke on a cold day?
5 Is there sufficient flow of fuel?
6 If not, are the filler cap breather and the fuel lines clear?
7 Is the petrol tap fully opened and is the tank full?
8 Are the carburettor internal passages clean?

If all these pass muster, on to the checks in the next section.

Loss of Power and Performance

Check the compression by kicking the engine over. If the compression is bad:

1 The cylinder head joint is leaking.
2 The sparking plug is not properly screwed in.
3 The piston or rings are damaged; or the rings are sticking in their grooves.

If the compression is good, the power loss can be caused by:

1 Slack big-end bearings.
2 Damaged rotary valve seating.
3 Seizure or wear on main bearings.
4 In the case of bearing trouble, the root cause may be use of the wrong grade of oil or insufficient oil.

Noise and Vibration

Vespa engines normally run quietly, and very smoothly. Excessive noise and/or vibration are indicative of trouble. The causes may be:

1 Running-in not properly carried out.
2 Overheating, caused by a build-up of dirt in the cooling fins or a damaged fan or cowl.
3 Sticking rings, leading to loss of compression and consequent overheating and bad starting.

4 Excessive carbon deposits, especially in the exhaust port and silencer. This could be due to the use of too much oil, or of a thicker grade than recommended.

Transmission Trouble

Any shortcomings in the clutch or gearbox are likely to be the result of actual damage to the parts themselves. Clutch snatch or slip and faulty operation of the gearbox may be due to improper lubrication. It is important to see that the gearbox oil does not fall below the correct level, since it feeds the gearbox, clutch and the clutch side main bearing.

Suspension Bottoming

There are two possible causes of bottoming on Vespa front suspension systems. They are:

1 Check the damper by bouncing the front of the machine. It should not oscillate. If it does, the damper may need replacing.
2 Check the rubber buffers.

Excessive Fuel Consumption

Carry out all the checks detailed on the ignition and carburation, and see that the engine compression is good and that there is no excessive carbon. Check also that the air intake is not blocked.

CHECK POINTS

These are the most important points to check when tracing troubles:

Engine. Tightness of nuts and bolts; grade of plug; grade and percentage of oil; contact-breaker gap; timing; setting of control cables.

Battery and lights. Conditions of rectifier; condition of fuse; security of terminal connections; battery connected correctly; insulation of leads intact and terminals unoxidized; bulb contacts clean and tight; horn regulating screw properly set.

Brakes. Controls properly set and working freely; brake drums unscored and not oval; brake shoes not excessively worn; oil seals in order.

Steering. Check the steering head bearing setting; listen for faulty bearing balls or "gritty" races; test the security of all wheel nuts; check the wheel bearings for play.

6 Engine removal and strip

APART from decarbonizing—for which there is no need to do more than swing the engine unit downwards—work on the Vespa engine/gearbox unit is best done on the workbench. This means detaching the unit from the frame—a relatively simple job, providing the following sequence is followed.

ENGINE REMOVAL

1 Undo the carburettor clamp, and ease the instrument from its stub.
2 Remove the silencer clamp bolt and the casing bolt. Detach the silencer.
3 Raise the machine on a stout box to give a foot or so of working clearance.
4 Undo one gear cable nipple screw at the selector end, and operate the twist grip control so that the other cable is loosened. Slide the cables clear.
5 Disconnect the clutch cable at the engine end.
6 Undo the bracket below the engine.
7 Remove the screw from the junction box near the kickstarter. Then disconnect the five cables at their terminals.
8 Engage gear, using the selector on the gearbox.
9 Detach the rear wheel and hub.
10 Remove the 14 mm bolt from the lower end of the damper.
11 Remove the 17 mm centre bolt from the engine pivot. The complete engine assembly can now be lifted from the machine.

Alternative method, for Decarbonizing

As stated above, there is no need to remove the engine simply for a decoke. Even so, to obtain clearance for removal of the barrel the unit must be swung out of place. The method is:

1 Undo the carburettor clamp, and ease the instrument from its stub.
2 Remove the silencer clamp bolt and casing bolt. Detach the silencer.
3 Remove the 14 mm bolt from the lower end of the damper.
4 Slacken—but do *not* remove—the 17 mm centre bolt in the engine pivot.

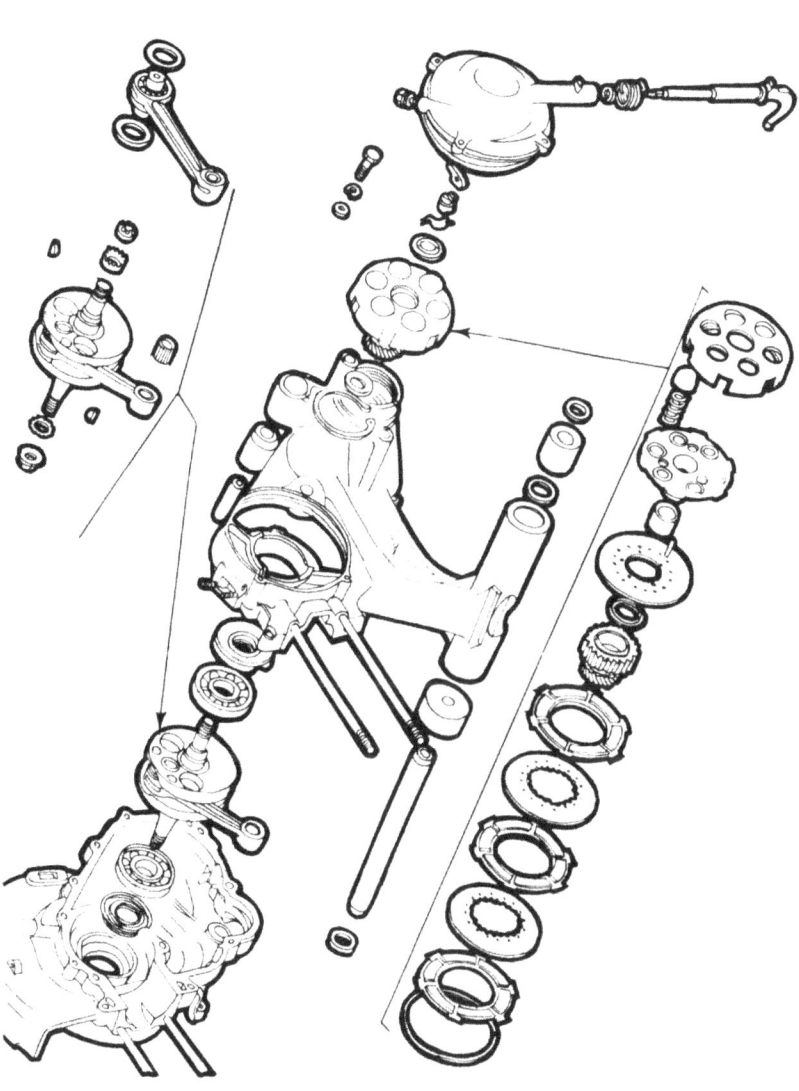

Fig. 5. The 125/150 Engine and Clutch "exploded." The relationship of the major components of the power unit

5 Swing the engine so that the head and barrel point downwards.
6 Remove the four nuts holding the head and barrel, and slide them from their studs.
7 Detach the gudgeon pin circlips and press out the pin. If it is tight warm the pistons for a minute or so by wrapping it in rag wrung out in hot water. This will expand it enough to free the pin.
8 Decarbonize the head, ports and piston crown. Check the rings and grooves.
9 When rebuilding, note that the piston crown is marked with an arrow. This *must* point towards the exhaust port. If the piston is refitted in any other position it will seize in the bore, since the ring gaps will run over the ports and become trapped. Double check this point before offering up the barrel on reassembly.

STRIPPING THE ENGINE UNIT

Provided proper care is exercised, and the right tools are used, there is no reason why the average private owner should not be able to overhaul his own Vespa engine. It is, however, essential to have a full set of Metric spanners (as described in Chapter 3) and to adhere rigidly to the sequence of work set out here.

It is also advisable to set aside, say, a week-end in which to do the complete job—it is surprising how much one can forget if a motor is left stripped for a week or two. If an interval is essential, it is no bad bet to label each part as it is removed and to place all components in boxes set out in removal sequence. This avoids any possibility of having to rebuild a unit from a heap of unfamiliar and unmarked parts!

Although it is not always done, my personal preference is also to clean the exterior of the unit thoroughly before dismantling starts. Using a top-quality grease solvent, such as Gunk, it is an easy matter to get the exterior clear of every scrap of dirt. It not only ensures that no grit is going to enter the internals—it also makes the work far more pleasant. There is nothing less conducive to enjoying mechanical work than having to handle filthy components.

The drill is simple. Brush the solvent all over the unit, getting it into every nook and cranny. Then hose it off with a gentle flow from a hose. Finish by mopping away all excess water—and any remaining dirt—with soft rag. You can then start the stripdown.

1 Remove the h.t. lead.
2 Remove the plug, and put it aside for sand-blasting and gapping.
3 Remove the four screws that hold the cowl. Two of these are on the offside; one is at the rear; and one is on the left.
4 Remove the three screws that secure the fan cover.
5 Undo the centre nut of the flywheel. Note that when you do this the

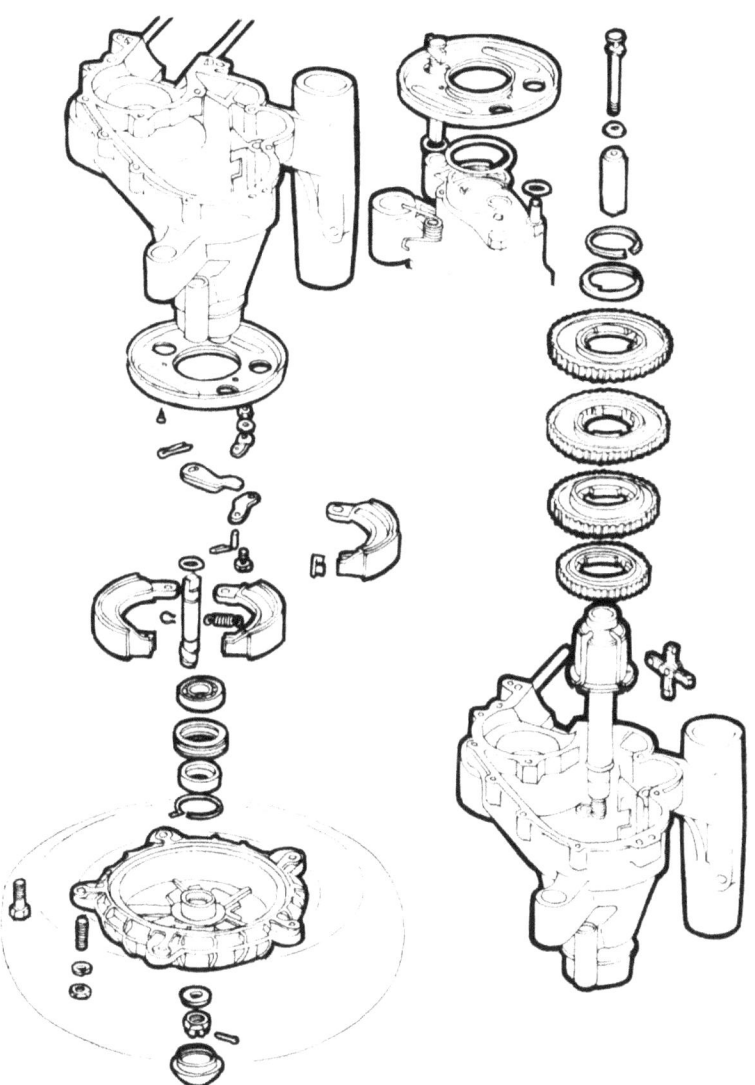

Fig. 6. The 125/150 Gearbox and Brake "exploded." How the component parts are arranged

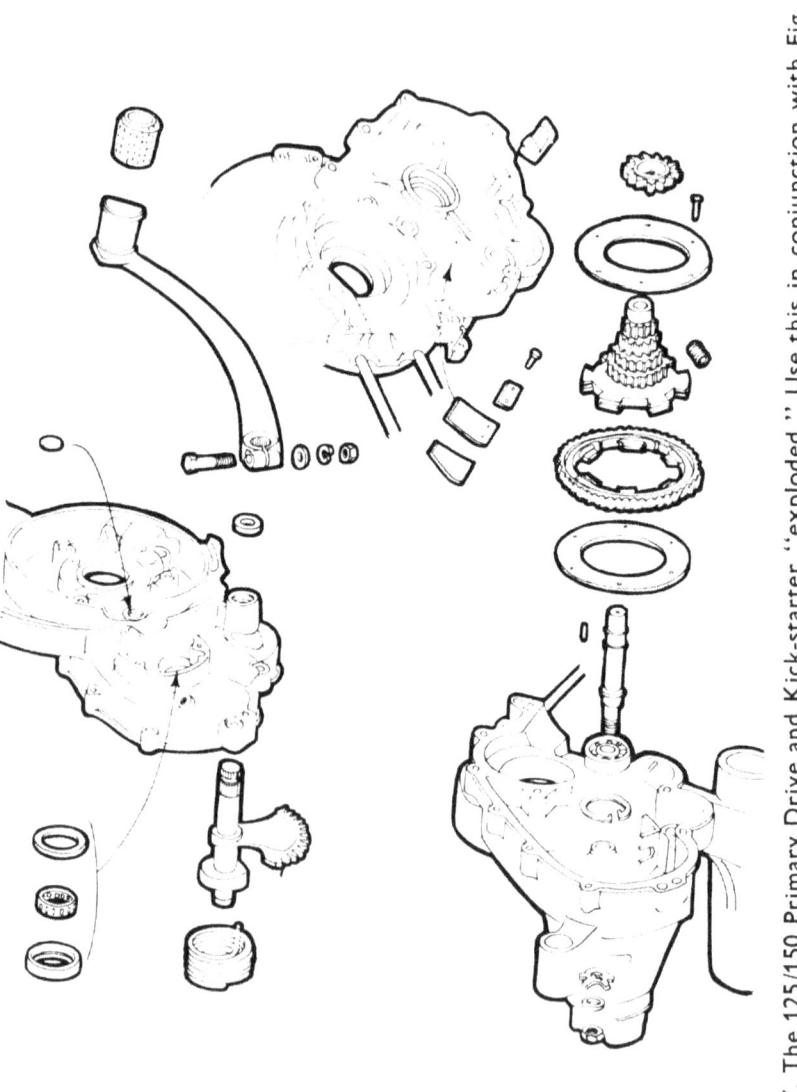

Fig. 7. The 125/150 Primary Drive and Kick-starter "exploded." Use this in conjunction with Fig. 6 for a full understanding of the transmission assembly

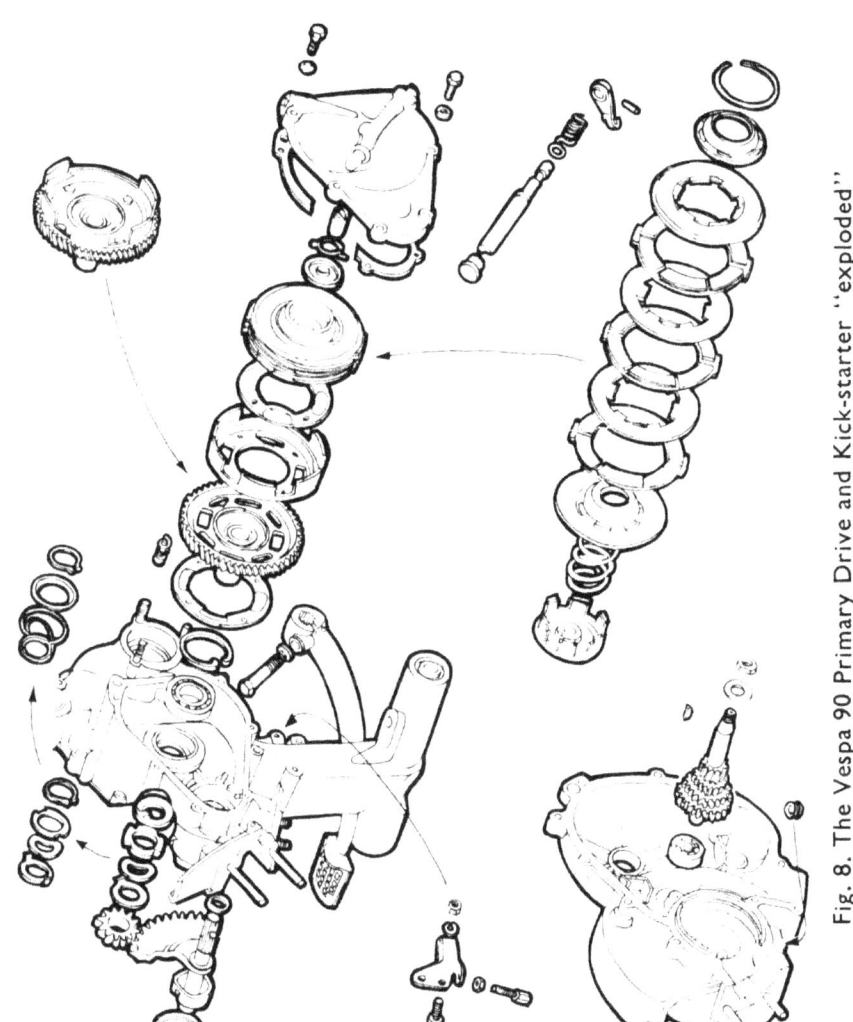

Fig. 8. The Vespa 90 Primary Drive and Kick-starter "exploded"

large circlip set in the flywheel must *not* be removed. It is there to help you detach the flywheel. The method is to fit a 14 mm box spanner over the nut, and insert a stout tommy bar. Use a club hammer to give the bar a sharp blow. This will break the taper, and the nut can be unscrewed—drawing the flywheel with it. Don't try to lock the flywheel with a screwdriver when freeing the nut—the result will simply be expensive damage. Get a friend to hold it steady while you hit the bar; but eschew mechanical locking.

6 With the flywheel off, the stator plate is exposed. So that you do not "lose" the timing, scribe matching marks on the edge of the stator and on the crankcase. That will enable you to refit it in exactly the same position when you come to rebuild. Now undo the three screws, with large washers, that hold the stator. Before attempting to pull it away from the crankcase, however, lightly grease the cable sleeves so that they will run easily through the grommets. The wiring harness passes through the top hole.

7 On the left of the unit, remove the small 8 mm screw that holds the brake drum.

8 Remove the split pin from the rear stub axle, and undo the 22 mm castellated nut on the hub. To prevent the hub turning, engage a gear; if necessary, temporarily refit the sparking plugs to provide compression. Normally, this should not be required. Once the nut is off, slide the hub off its spines.

9 Remove the three nuts holding the brake back plate. On earlier models these were 10 mm; on later ones, 14 mm. The brake plate, complete with shoes, can then be detached.

10 Undo the ring of six 10 mm bolts that secure the clutch cover. Take off the cover, the cover gasket, and the thrust pad.

11 Flatten the tab washer under the clutch centre nut and undo the nut with a 17 mm spanner. Take off the washer, and use a puller to remove the complete clutch. An alternative method is to remove the head and barrel, and then undo the bolts holding the crankcase half. With that detached, the clutch can be driven out, using a soft-metal drift.

12 Detach the barrel and head, secure by four nuts.

13 Eleven bolts and two nuts hold the timing side of the crankcase. Remove these, and pull away the case. The layshaft will come with it.

14 Remove the large circlip on the mainshaft and take off the spacing washers and gears. As you do so, make a careful note of their relative positions as an aid to reassembly.

15 Drive out the kickstarter quadrant shaft and spring, using a mallet, from the left-hand side. Note that there is a rubber sealing ring in the kickstarter spindle hole. This *must* be sound.

16 Lift out the ratchet assembly.

17 Undo the circlip securing the clutch centre. Detach the clutch shaft—flatten the tab washer and remove the 19 mm centre nut.

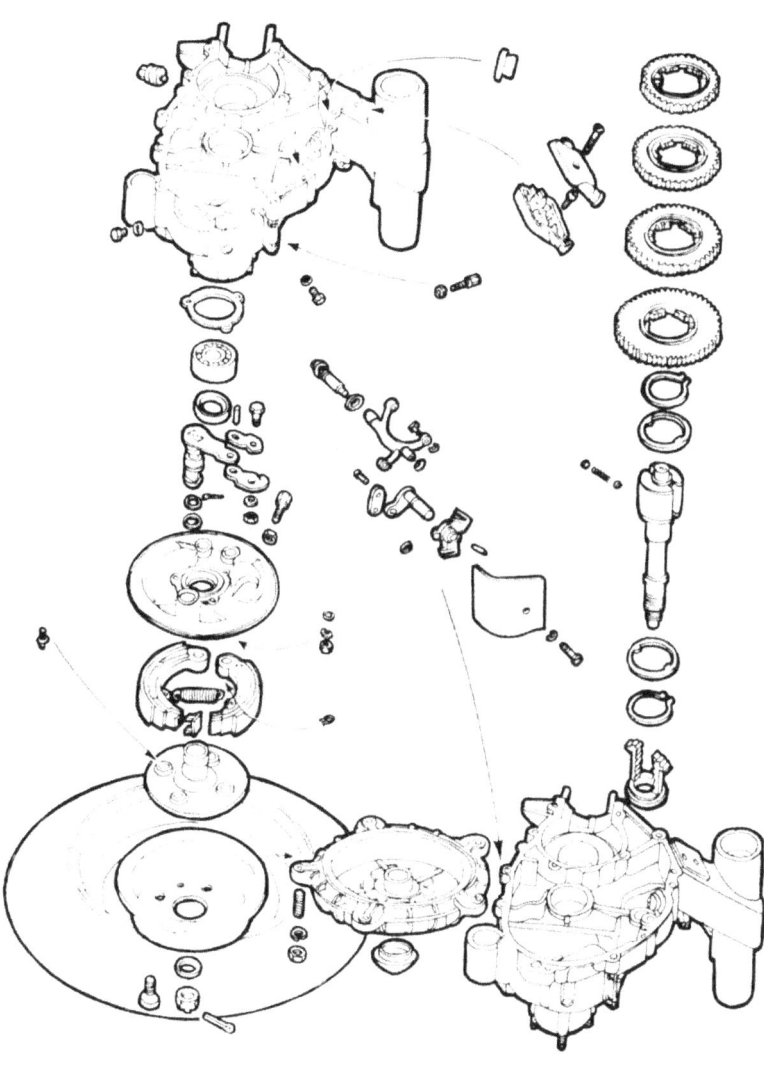

Fig. 9. The Vespa 90 Gearbox and Rear Brake "exploded"

This is the "official" sequence. It may, however, be easier to carry out this part of the job if it is done immediately after Stage 11, *before* detaching the barrel and head.

18 Next, line up the wide slot on the clutch body—there are six slots all told—with the pinion. This enables the gear to be removed.
19 Lift out the crankshaft.
20 Set the wide slot on the clutch body over the main shaft. Use a mallet to drive out the shaft, supporting it as you do so.
21 Next, turn the wide slot to the casting mark at the base of the case. Lift it outwards and turn it to the rear to withdraw it.
22 The main bearing has an oil seal in the inside. Remove the seal, detach the circlip, and tap out the bearing.
23 A circlip also retains the clutch shaft bearing. Remove this, and tap out the bearing.
24 Warm the casing, and tap out the main shaft bearing.
25 To reach the selector fork, remove the screw holding the cover.
26 A special tool *must* be used to remove the outer track of the timing side bearing. If this requires renewal, take the casing to your local Vespa dealer. The same applies to the mainshaft timing side bearing.
27 To remove the layshaft bearing, again warm the case until the bearing can be tapped out.
28 If it is necessary to change the selector cruciform in the mainshaft, remove the circlip and pull the selector towards the splined end of the shaft. Take care not to lose the two balls and the spring that will be released as the selector comes clear.

When reassembling this unit, make up a pair of wooden formers about six inches long, notched at one end to match the balls. Grease the balls and the spring, and insert them. Use the notched formers to hold them in place as the cruciform is driven on.

ENGINE REASSEMBLY

In general, reassembly of the engine unit should proceed in reverse order from dismantling. There are several points to note, however.

1 The clutch centre goes in first, using the wide slot to allow clearance for insertion. It will only fit in this one position—and even then a certain amount of "knack" is required.
2 Mount the gears on the mainshaft before offering it up to the gearbox. They fit thus:
   1st Concave side inwards.
   2nd and 3rd Flush faces inwards.
   4th Flat face outwards.

Check that there is a space between each pinion. *If the faces rub together at any point, then the assembly is wrong.* Note, too, that the trunnions

ENGINE REMOVAL AND STRIP

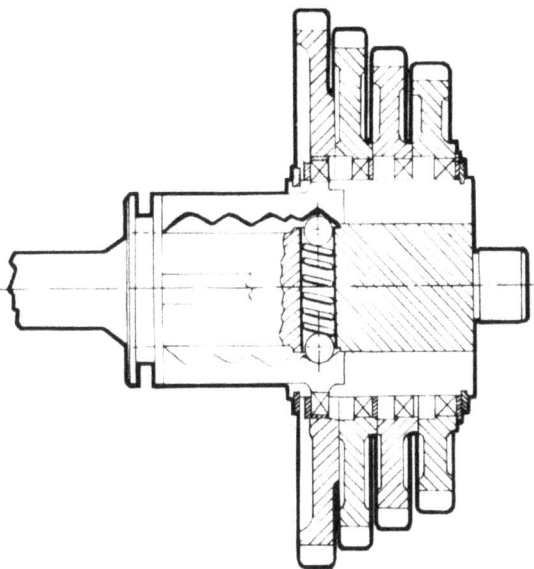

Fig. 10. Correct assembly for the Gear Cluster. Rebuild the cluster so that the dished faces fall in this sequence

on the selector must be properly engaged in their track on the selector ring before the mainshaft goes home. The shaft can be tapped into position (a workshop would use a special tool) but this must not be overdone or the bearing will be disturbed.

3 To refit the kickstarter assembly, offer up the ratchet and fit the quadrant. Push the spring tongue into the hole on the front of the boss. Then lift it round until the other tongue engages in the slot on the anchorage on the quadrant.

7 Carburettor service

COMPARED with the instruments used on cars—with their masses of jets, pumps and butterflies—the Vespa's carburettor looks and is simple. But it is also efficient and reliable, and there should normally be no need to disturb it.

In time, however, the impurities that are present in every gallon of petrol that you buy will accumulate in the float chamber, and the carburettor will need to be cleaned. Once a year should be ample.

This is the stripping technique, after removal of the air cleaner and heat baffle:

1 Remove the carburettor, and free it from the machine by disconnecting the fuel pipe and the control assemblies.

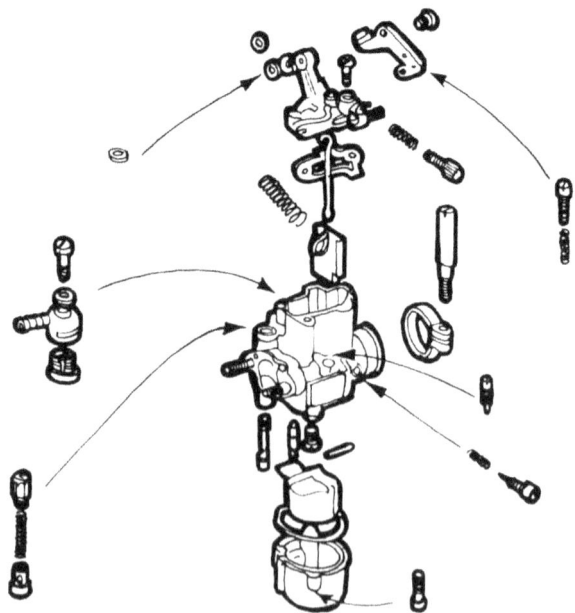

Fig. 11. The Vespa 90 Carburettor "exploded"

CARBURETTOR SERVICE

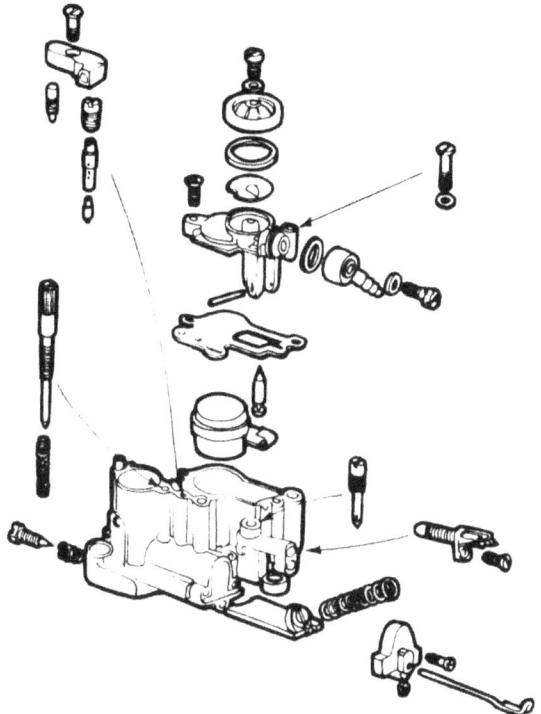

Fig. 12. The Vespa 125/150 Carburettor "exploded"

The throttle cable and rocker are fixed to the mixing chamber top (held by screws). So is the throttle slide. When the screws are removed, the whole assembly can be pulled away. Forward of the fuel intake is the starting jet complex, consisting of a cable adjuster, with a spring and plunger below it. Undo the adjuster and slide the plunger from the housing.

2 Unscrew the slow-running jet, set on the left-hand side just above the float chamber. It has a slotted head. Blow through it to clean it; then refit it.

3 Open up the float chamber, which is held by two screws. Note that there is a rubber sealing ring inserted in the groove around the chamber.

4 Unscrew and clean the main jet, set in the bottom of the jet tube. A tyre pump will give a blast of air sufficient to clear the jet.

5 At the front, on the float pivot side, is the starting jet itself. Again, remove this and clean it with a blast of air.

6 Remove the float by pressing out its pivot pin. Lift the float. The needle that controls the fuel flow will come away with it, complete with its nylon seating.

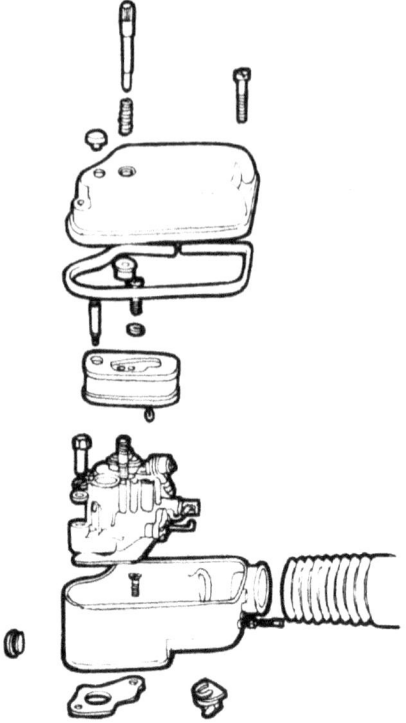

Fig. 13. The Air Cleaner layout, Vespa 125/150

7 On the fuel intake there is a nylon filter, held by a single screw. Remove this, and wash the filter in clean petrol.
8 Wash out the float chamber with clean petrol to remove all grit, etc. Check the float for damage, and ensure that the needle is not bent or pitted.
9 Reassemble the carburettor in the reverse order to that used for stripping. When doing so, be careful to refit the gasket between the air filter and the intake so that it is the right way round. Failure to do this will result in the slow-running bleed hole being blanked off by the gasket. This will ruin engine idling. The hole in the gasket *must* match up with air-bleed aperture.

Before refitting the carburettor, clean the air filter. When the instrument is back on the scooter, adjust the idling by *gently* screwing in the mixture screw, which is set horizontally behind the top edge of the float chamber, on the right-hand side. It must just—but only just—be fully home. Too much force will damage its seating. Then open it by $1\frac{1}{2}$ turns. It is now properly set.

CARBURETTOR SERVICE

The desired idling speed must now be obtained by raising or lowering the throttle slide, using the throttle stop screw on top of the slide-operating rocker.

Fuel tap. It is impossible to remove the fuel tap without using the special T 0021064 spanner that is necessary to reach the internal securing nut inside the tank. This has a flexible shank, with jaws set at right angles to it. Unless you can borrow this tool, it is better to refer this job to your local Vespa agent.

8 Care of the electrics

WHETHER or not your particular model has the refinement of a battery, its electrical equipment follows a basic pattern that has been well tried over many years.

The heart of the system is a flywheel magneto-generator, driven direct by the crankshaft. The magneto section produces the high-tension current to provide the spark at the plug points. The generator produces low-tension electricity which can be used direct to light up the bulbs and operate the horn or—through a rectifier—to charge a battery that provides current for the job.

With all electrical systems, maintenance is normally confined to very simple tasks. The sparking plug must be kept clean and properly gapped. So, too, must the contact-breaker points in the magneto. All electrical leads must be properly insulated and secured; and all connections must be tight and clean, so that resistance to the flow of current is kept to a minimum. The only major job is to ensure that the timing is correct, for on this hinges both the performance and the economy of the machine.

CHECKING AND ADJUSTING THE TIMING

With a new scooter, the timing has been accurately set at the factory and no alteration should be necessary. With a secondhand model it's a different story—some previous owner may well have tampered with the settings. If the performance is not up to average, a timing check will do no harm— and it may transform the scooter. But follow this sequence carefully.

Start by making up a simple test lamp, using a 1·5 volt torch battery, a suitable bulb, and a pair of "jumper" leads. These are simply lengths of insulated electrical wire equipped with crocodile clips at one end, and wired to the test lamp.

Then open up the engine cowling and remove the inspection plate so that you can reach the internals of the flywheel. Take out the sparking plug so that it is easier to turn the engine, and ensure that the gear is in neutral. Now proceed as follows:

1 Turn the flywheel until one of the magnets is immediately above the ignition coil, which is set at the top of the unit.
2 Check the distance between the front edge of the coil shoe and the

CARE OF THE ELECTRICS 43

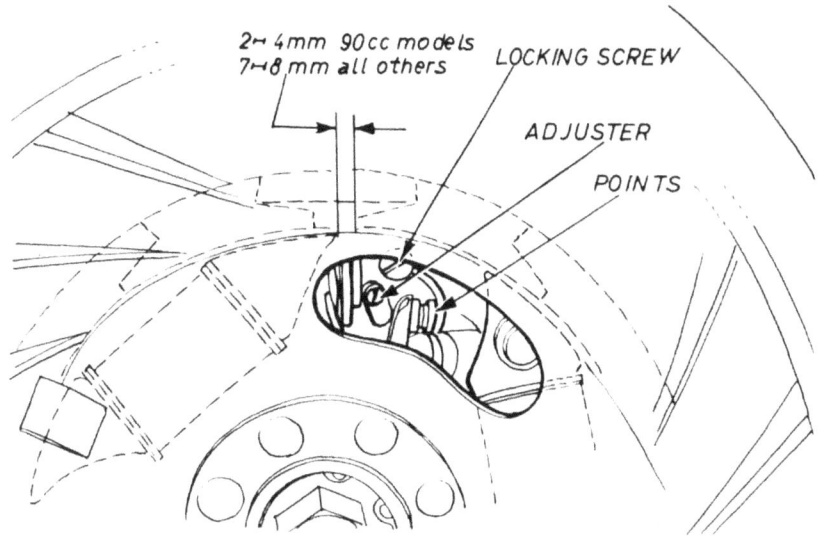

Fig. 14. Ignition Timing Adjustment, all models

edge of the *next* magnet. This must be 5/64–5/32 in. (4–8 mm) on all models except the 90s, where the correct measurement is 1/32–5/64 in. (2–4 mm).

3 Now rig the test lamp, connecting one of its crocodile clips to the red lead from the magneto, and the other to the black. This is, in fact, connecting across the fixed contact point and earth. Loosen the screw holding the fixed point, and turn the eccentric adjusting screw on the points plate until the points are just breaking. Use the timing lamp as your guide. While the points are together it stays out; as they open, it lights up.

4 Retighten the locking screw and rotate the flywheel until the points are fully open. Then check the gap with a feeler gauge. It should be within the range of 0·011 and 0·019 in.

5 If the correct readings have not been obtained by this method, it will be necessary to use a degree plate to make a new setting. You can buy one through an accessory shop. It is simply an oversized circular protractor. Fix the degree plate to the flywheel, and attach a pointer— a piece of hooked wire trapped under a bolt head will suffice—to the crankcase.

6 Now you have to find TDC accurately. To do this, use a blunt screwdriver. Insert it through the plug hole and hold it still while you turn the flywheel. When you feel the piston touch the end of the screwdriver, stop turning and make a pencil mark on the degree plate at the

setting indicated by the pointer. Keep the screwdriver absolutely still and turn the flywheel in reverse until the piston again touches the screwdriver. Mark this second point as well. Remove the screwdriver, and check the number of degrees between the two marks. A setting exactly halfway between them will give you precise TDC.

7 Use the test lamp in conjunction with the degree plate to check the point at which the contacts open. It should be 28° BTDC on 150 c.c. Standard and Sportique models; 25° ± 1° on the 125 c.c. VMA 1; or 19° ± 1° on the 90 range.

8 If adjustment is needed, the flywheel will have to be removed and the stator turned slightly in relation to the crankcase. Before you loosen the screws that secure it, however, scribe matching marks on the stator and the case so that you have a reference point. You will already know, from the readings taken on the timing disc, by how many degrees the timing is out. You can use the disc—or a protractor —to indicate the position to which the stator must be moved to correct the timing. Make a soft-pencil mark the requisite number of degrees from the datum mark you have scribed. Remember that if the engine is over-advanced the stator will have to be turned clockwise to the right setting. If it is retarded, it will have to go anti-clockwise.

9 Loosen the stator screws, turn the plate to the new mark, and tighten the screws again. Slip the flywheel on to the shaft, and recheck the advance. If it is now within limits, tighten down the flywheel nut. If not, remove the flywheel and make a second adjustment to get the setting absolutely correct.

Effect of Worn Points

A word of warning is due here—if the gap that was recorded during the "phasing" of the points (in steps 1–4) was less than 0·011 or more than 0·019 in. the inference is that new points are essential. Almost without doubt, the fibre heel of the moving arm has become badly worn, or the fixed bracket may be bent.

To remove the points, take off the flywheel, and pull away the circlip that holds the moving point to the fixed pivot. Undo and remove the screw clamping the points plate to the stator, and lift the points set outwards. Undo the single nut and bolt holding the electrical connections to the points plate, making a careful note of the sequence of the plain and insulating washers. The bolt is mounted head downwards. Next to the head is a plain washer. Next comes an insulating washer, and after that the insulating sleeve that passes round the hollow pin on the moving contact-return spring. Above this goes a second insulating washer, followed by the electrical leads, a plain washer, and the nut. Get the insulating washers where the plain ones should be—and vice versa—and the ignition system will be most effectively short-circuited!

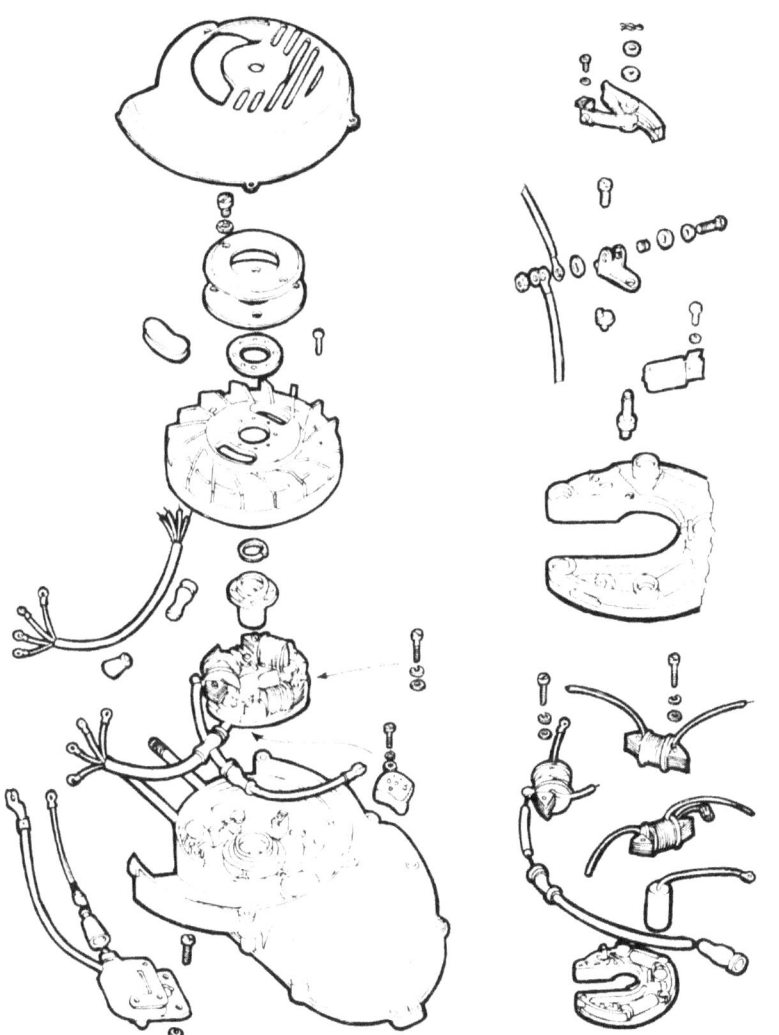

Fig. 15. The Vespa 90 Generator

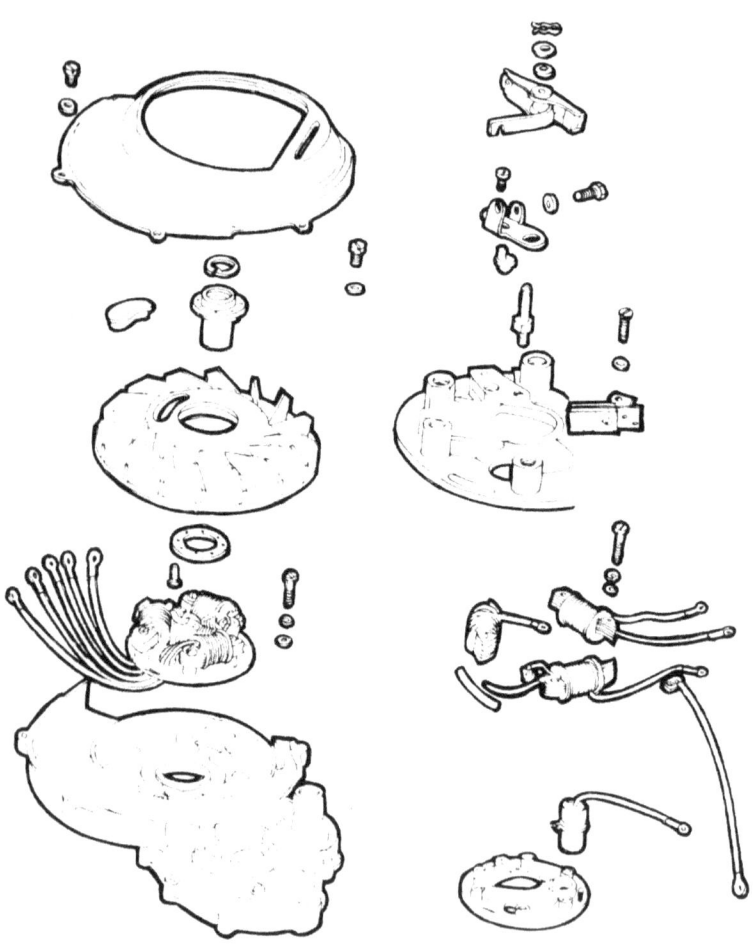

Fig. 16. The Vespa 125/150 Generator

Cleaning and Facing Points

Arcing across the points eventually results in a "pip" forming on one contact and a hollow on the other. The contacts can also become wedge-shaped instead of cylindrical. Both faults can be corrected by refacing the contacts on a stone or dressing them with a points file, although severely worn points are best renewed.

Where the problem is asymmetric wear, grind or file away the contacts until they will meet squarely. Where there is a "pip," remove it. Then dress both surfaces to get even contact—but do not try to file away enough material to remove the hollow. It has no practical effect and can safely be left.

Clean the contacts with petrol, and dry them before refitting.

BATTERY CARE

A battery on a machine that is not in regular use can discharge itself in a month. In such cases, it is best to remove it and have it professionally recharged. In most instances, the charging rate must not exceed one ampere—and the garage should be reminded of this. Most home trickle-chargers exceed this rate, so if buying one check first that it will be suitable for the job. Some designs are self-sensing and automatically adjust themselves to the battery's requirements. Others (made mainly for car use) charge at a fixed rate of around 4 amps and would "cook" a scooter-sized battery.

Even where the battery is receiving a regular charge from use of the machine, it should be removed at intervals of a month so that the terminals can be cleaned and the specific gravity checked with a hydrometer. "Dry" batteries, that use a jelly-type electrolyte, should have a teaspoonful of distilled water added to each cell. They are then allowed to stand for fifteen minutes, after which any excess moisture must be siphoned or shaken out. This work should only be done immediately after a trip has been made.

With "wet" batteries, in which the electrolyte is a dilute acid, a very different method is employed. Each cell is checked to ensure that the level inside is just over the top of the separators between the plates. If not, enough distilled water is poured in to obtain this level. The cells are self-contained, so the check must be made individually on each. If too much distilled water is added inadvertently, *never* try to pour it out. And *never* invert a wet battery—the result will be acid everywhere! To drain off surplus electrolyte, insert a short length of plastic tube into the cell and immerse it. Place a thumb over the open end and lift the tube away. The suction will have trapped a small amount of electrolyte in the tube, which will not be released until you raise your thumb from the aperture.

A fully-charged battery, at 60 F air temperature, will have electrolyte at a specific gravity of 1·270–1·290. At 1·200 the battery is virtually discharged, and above 1·300 it probably has damaged plates.

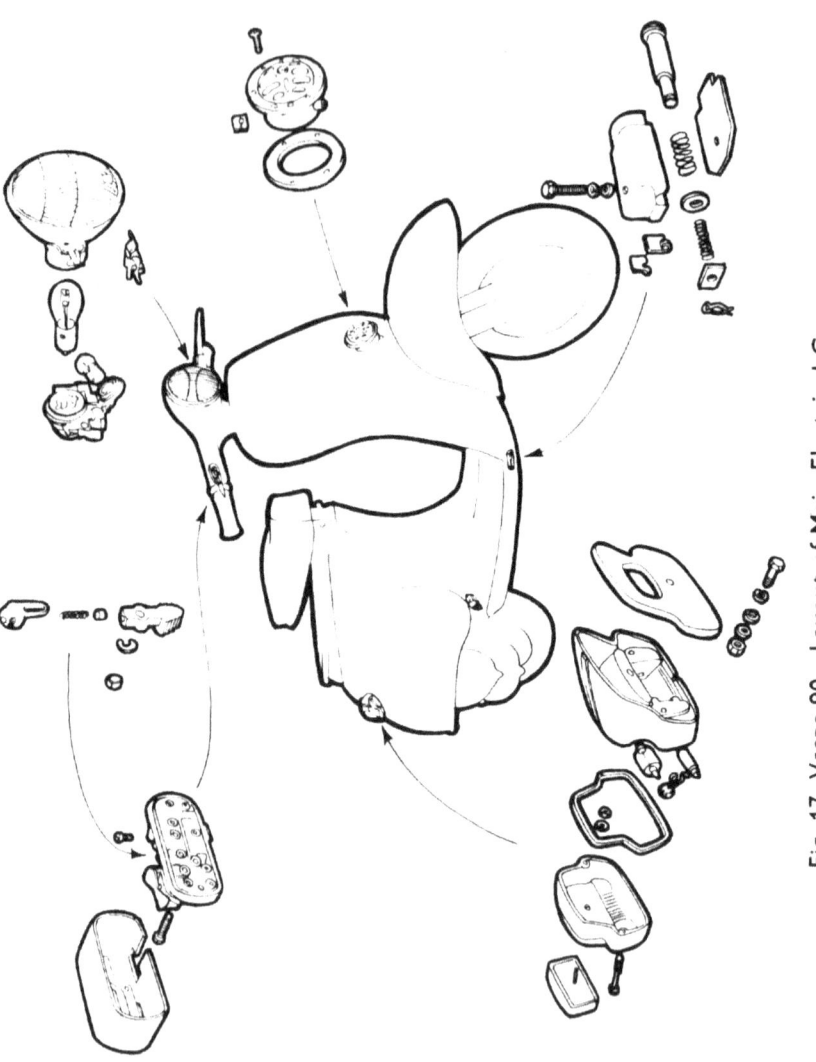

Fig. 17. Vespa 90—Layout of Main Electrical Components

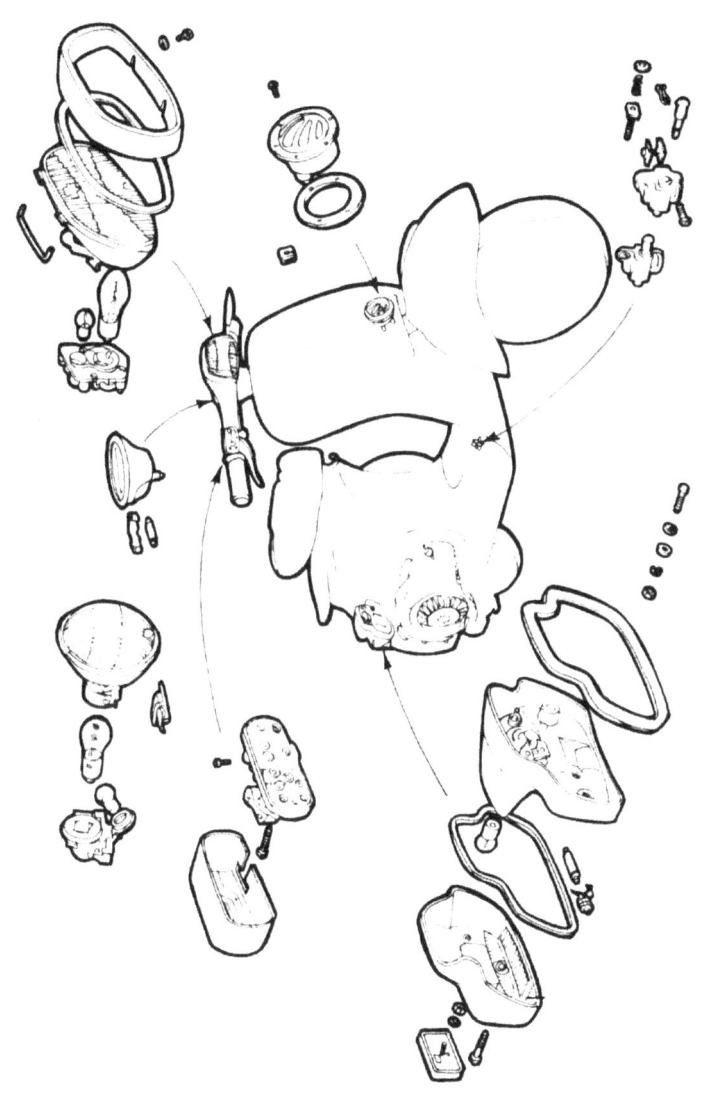

Fig. 18. Vespa 125/150—Layout of Main Electrical Components

Hydrometer measurements are made by immersing the hydrometer in each cell in turn, and drawing up a sample by pressing and releasing the bulb. An internal float then registers the specific gravity. This check should not be made immediately after topping up, or a false reading will result.

BULBS AND LOOM

At least once every year—better still, twice; just before and just after the winter—it pays to remove all bulbs and check their contacts. In use, a thin film of corrosion builds up on these. It acts as an electrical resistance and reduces the efficiency of the system.

Use fine emery cloth to rub contacts of the bulb and the lamp holder to bright metal, so that a first-rate electrical connection results. Look, also, for signs of blackening on the glass "envelope" of the bulb. This is a sign that the filament is weakening and may shortly blow. One sure (but drastic) test is to tap the bulb sharply with a snap of your fingers. On a faulty one, it will break the filament there and then. You will, of course, then need a new bulb—but that is better than having a sudden black-out one dark night.

Work on the actual wiring loom entails nothing more complicated than carrying out an inspection to make sure that all insulation is sound and that every wire is properly attached at its terminals. Repair any scuffing on the insulation, using a couple of turns of insulating tape. And check each terminal carefully, tightening up where necessary.

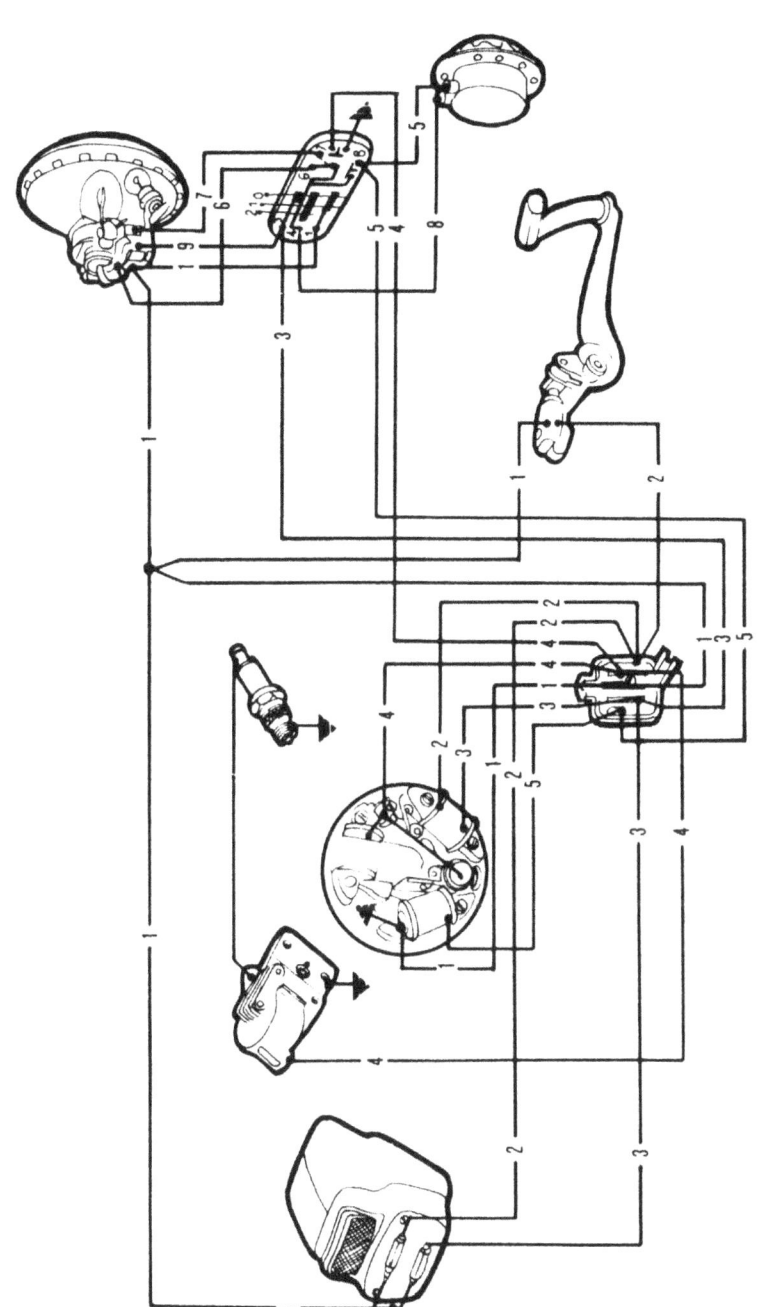

Fig. 19. Visual Wiring Diagram—Vespa 90S. The code numbers are for lead tracing only

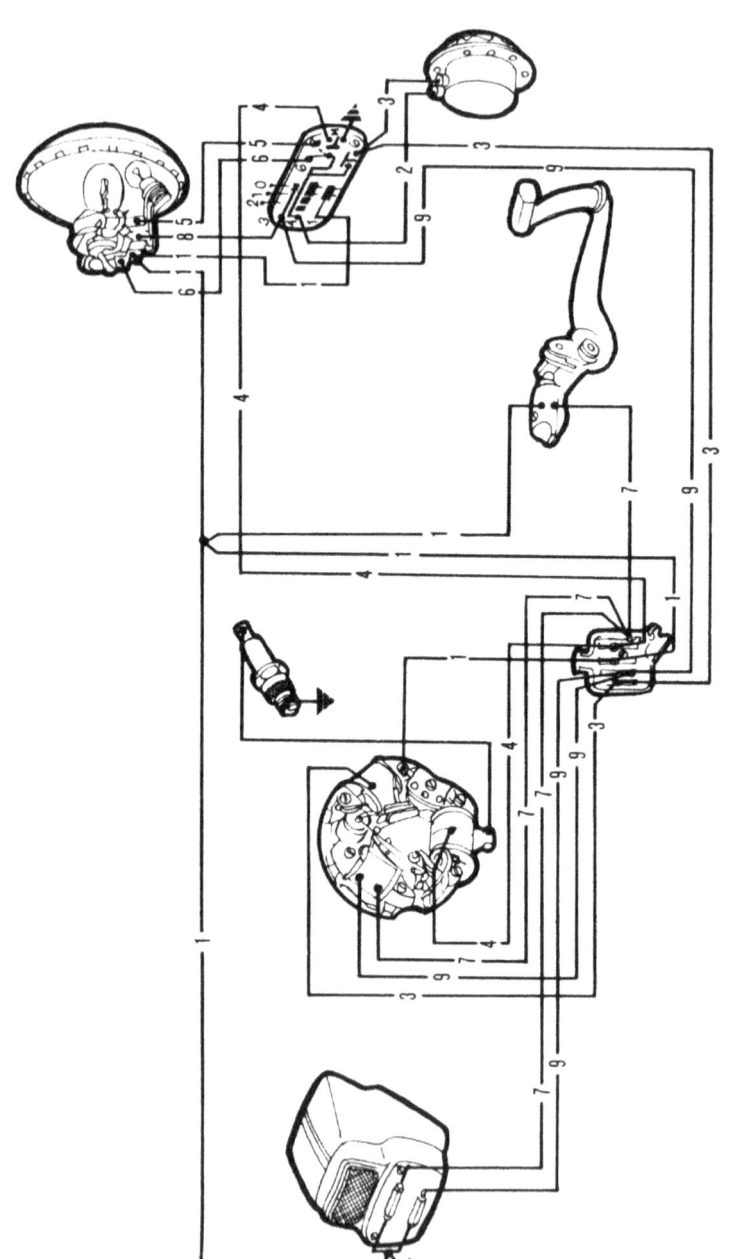

Fig. 20. Visual Wiring Diagram, Vespa 90. The code numbers are for lead tracing only

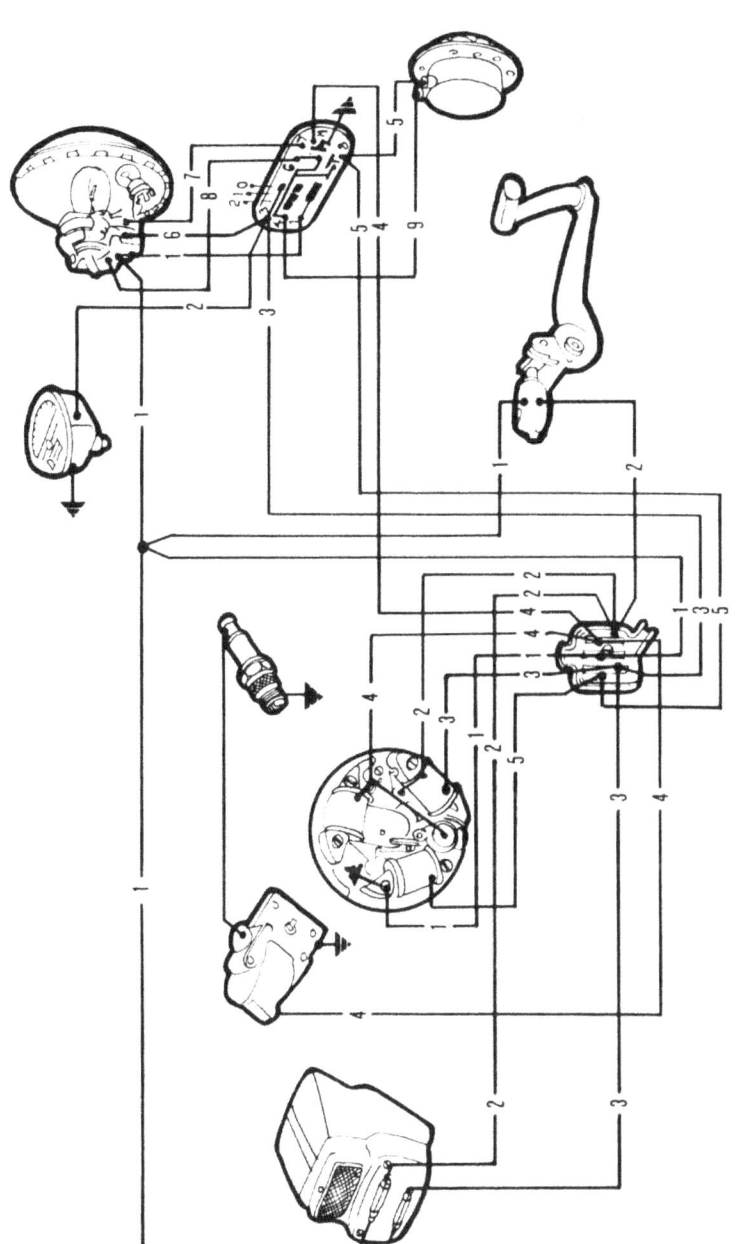

Fig. 21. Visual Wiring Diagram, Vespa 125. The code numbers are for lead tracing only

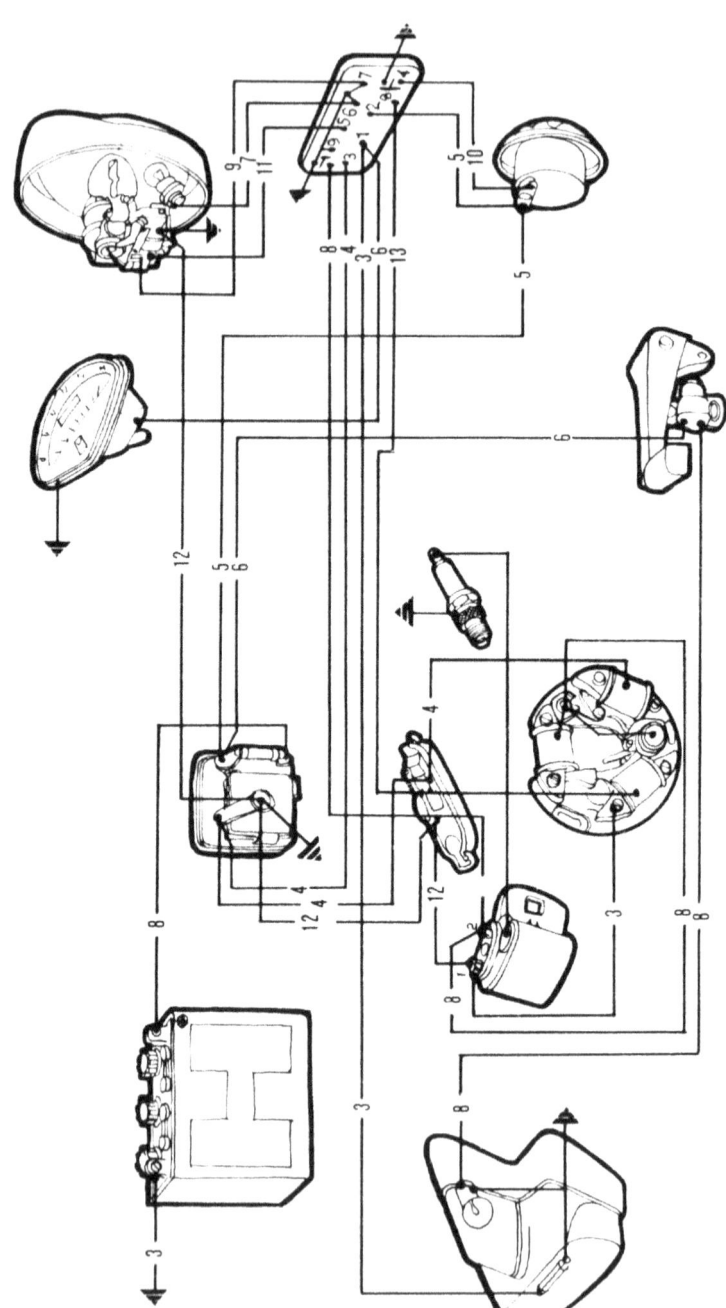

Fig. 22. Visual Wiring Diagram Vespa 150. The code numbers are for lead tracing only

9 Suspension, brakes and controls

With its car-like body structure obviating a separate frame; the engine/transmission unit "doubling" as a rear suspension arm; and an overhung axle at the front, there is little on the Vespa that follows the conventional motorcycle frame and suspension concept.

So far as the rear suspension is concerned, all necessary steps for dismantling have already been detailed in the engine removal sequence described in Chapter 6. Steps 7–9 in that sequence also fully describe the stripping of the rear brake.

Front Brake, V9A 1

To remove the front brake on this model, take out the nylon plug that is set in the wheel link. Then undo the brass plug on the speedo drive and pull out the skew drive gear.

The gear drive cover is also the spindle nut. Detach it—it has a left-hand thread. Then withdraw the axle, and apart from removal of the shoes your brake is dismantled for servicing.

Front Brake, all other Models

On all other Vespas, front brake removal involves detaching the alloy cap over the hub to give access to the axle nut. This is of castellated type, locked by a split pin.

Straighten out the pin (use a new one on reassembly) and pull it away. Undo the nut, and pull the complete hub assembly from the stub axle. The shoes are now exposed.

Brake Shoe Removal and Replacement

To remove brake shoes, turn the operating lever until both shoes are riding on the edge of the cam. Then remove the circlips holding the shoes to the fixed posts. Insert a screwdriver under each shoe in turn, at a point close to the cam, and prise them off.

To refit shoes, first join each pair with its spring. Place them on the backplate, engaging them with the cam but not attempting—at this stage—to fit them to the posts. Turn the operating lever so that the cam expands the shoes. Then fit each shoe in turn over its pivot, and replace the circlips.

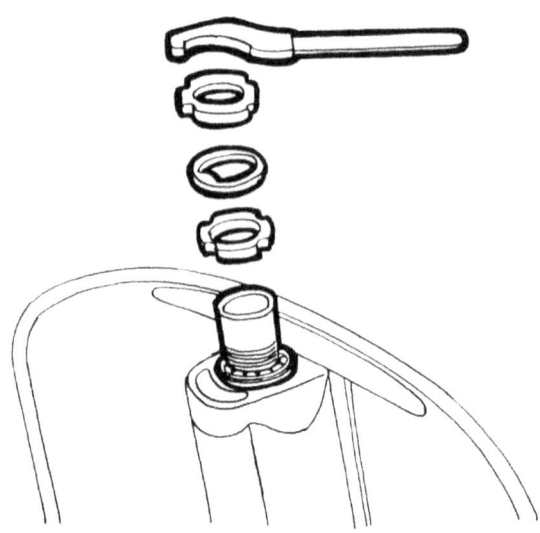

Fig. 23. Steering Head Bearing, all models. Use a C-spanner (shown top) to turn the rings when carrying out adjustments or when dismantling

Head Bearing Adjustment

All Vespas use a conventional steering head with ball bearings at top and bottom. Adjustment is effected by loosening the upper slotted locking ring, using a C-spanner (Tool No. 0014566) and then turning the lower slotted adjuster ring clockwise to tighten the bearings, anti-clockwise to loosen them.

The adjustment must be such that when the front of the scooter is blocked up the forks will swing freely from lock to lock, with no tight spots. At the same time, there must be no fore-and-aft play on the forks. When this setting has been found, the locking ring is retightened to hold it. Afterwards, check that the setting was not disturbed during this operation.

Front Fork Removal

Start by blocking up the scooter with the front wheel 18 in. off the ground. Remove the headlamp. This gives access to the speedo drive, which must be unscrewed from the speedo head. Next, disconnect the front brake cable at the wheel end and free the single bolt (which may have either a 13 mm or 14 mm head) at the handlebar clamp. By lifting on the bars, the complete handlebar unit (with its controls still connected) can be eased off the stem and pivoted forward to hang in front of the machine.

Completely remove the locking ring from the stem. Insert a block under

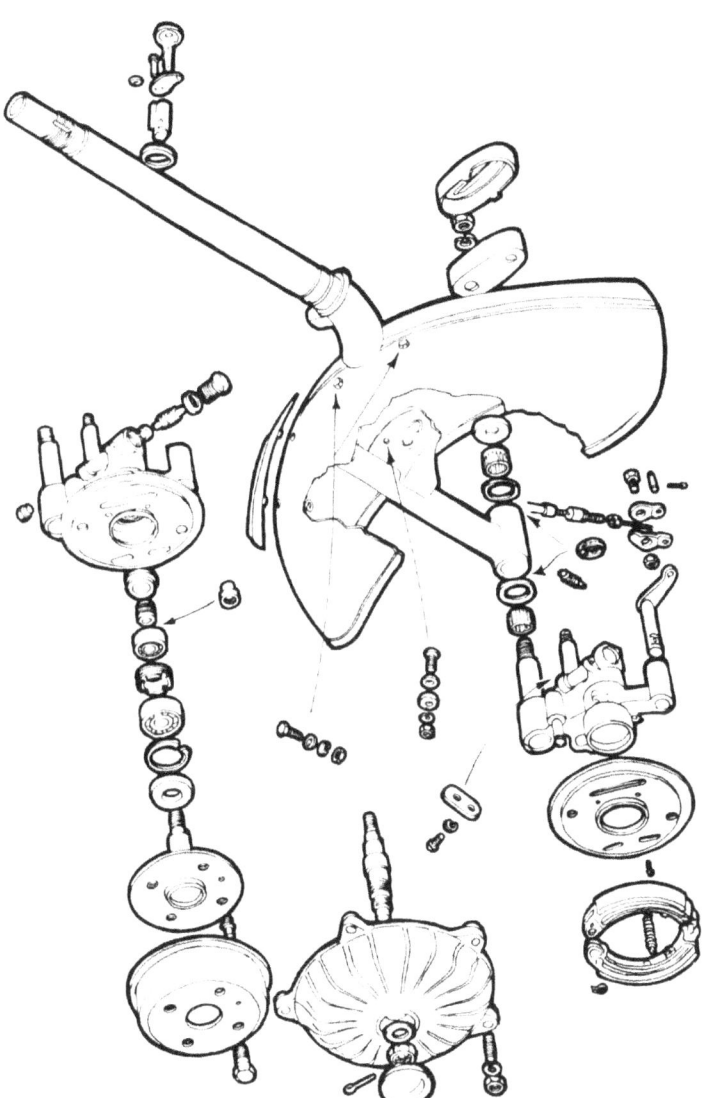

Fig. 24. Vespa 90 Front Forks and Front Brake "exploded"

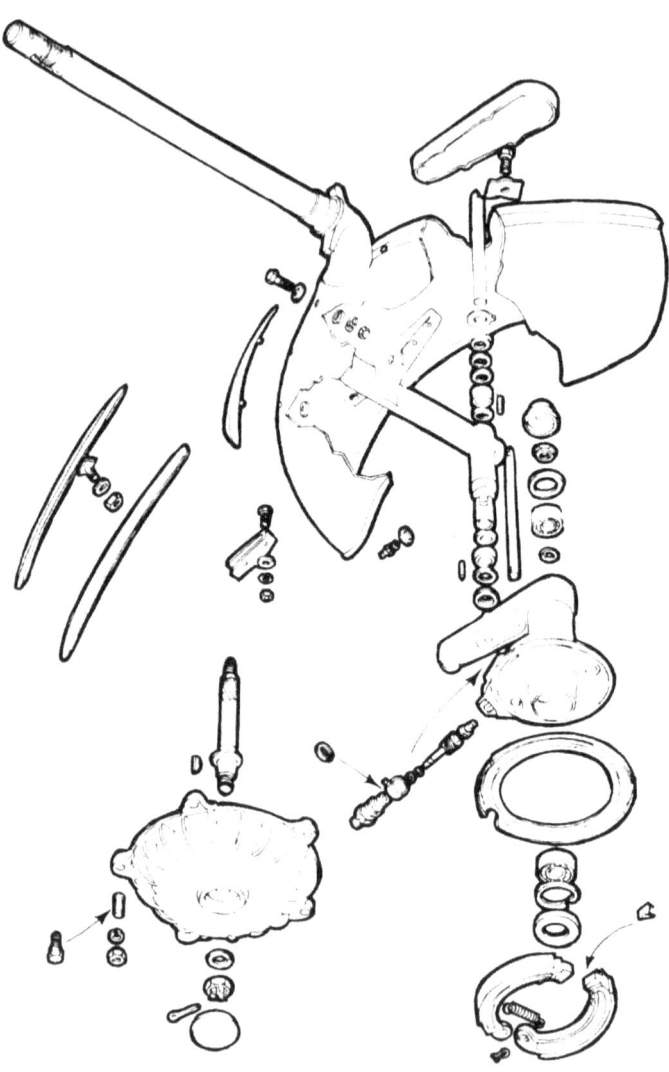

Fig. 25. Vespa 125/150 Front Forks and Front Brake "exploded"

SUSPENSION, BRAKES AND CONTROLS

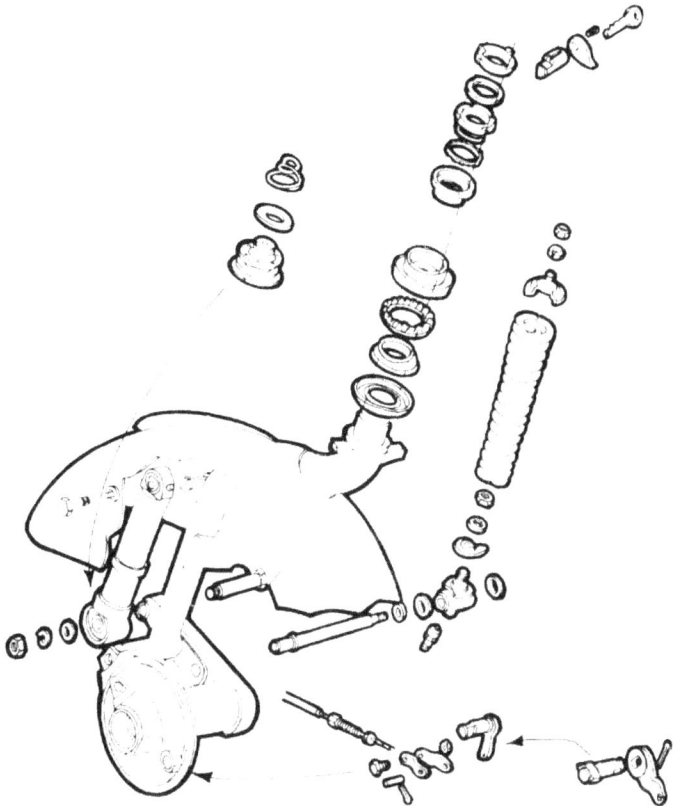

Fig. 26. Vespa 125/150 Front Fork Damper and Spring Layout

the front wheel so that the forks cannot drop, and remove the adjuster ring. Hold the forks, remove the wheel block, and withdraw the fork unit downwards to clear the stem from the steering head. Take care not to lose the bearing balls.

Inspect the upper and lower bearing tracks that remain in the head. Damaged tracks can be driven out by use of a long soft-metal drift and mallet, the drift being inserted from the reverse end of the head. To remove the lower track and dust cover from the stem, a special extractor is employed (T.0016561). In its absence, a damaged track can be driven off by tapping around its lower surface with a soft-metal drift and mallet until it comes clear.

Fork Link Removal

Take off the wheel and brake drum and remove the brake shoes. Detach the hydraulic damper by undoing its upper and lower securing bolts. Then release the two nuts that hold the spring. The upper nut is on top of the

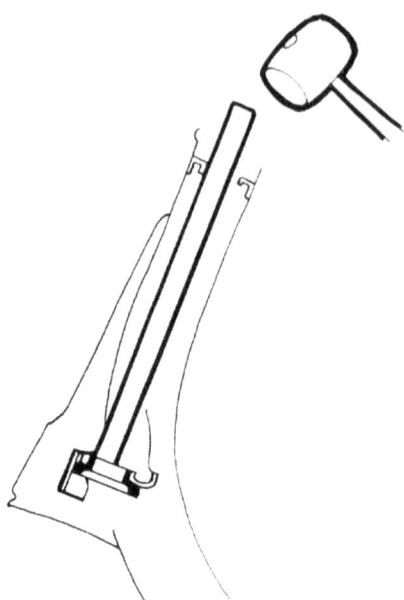

Fig. 27. All models—removal of Lower Steering Head Bearing. This bearing can only be detached by using a long soft-metal drift and a hammer to drive it out from above

spring mounting welded to the fork leg. The lower one is on the inner face of the spring trunnion on the link itself.

The pivot pin for the link can be one of two designs; either with a single 17 mm nut hidden below the detachable link cover, or with a locking plate and bolt. Removal of the nut or bolt enables the pin to be driven out through the fork pivot.

Needle roller bearings are used in the pivot on later models, and plain phospor-bronze bushes on earlier types. Either can be driven out from the opposite side, using a long soft-metal drift and mallet. Reassembly is simply a reversal of dismantling.

Control Cables

The extremely clean design of the Vespa handlebar is due in no small measure to the concealment of the various control cables—clutch, gear change, throttle and brake—all of which pass through the central spine and thus up, beside the stem, into the nacelle.

In the event of cable breakage there is a set routine for replacement. Pulling the cable out means that the entire steering will have to be dismantled; and it *is* possible to avoid this.

The simplest method is to withdraw just the inner cable, leaving the

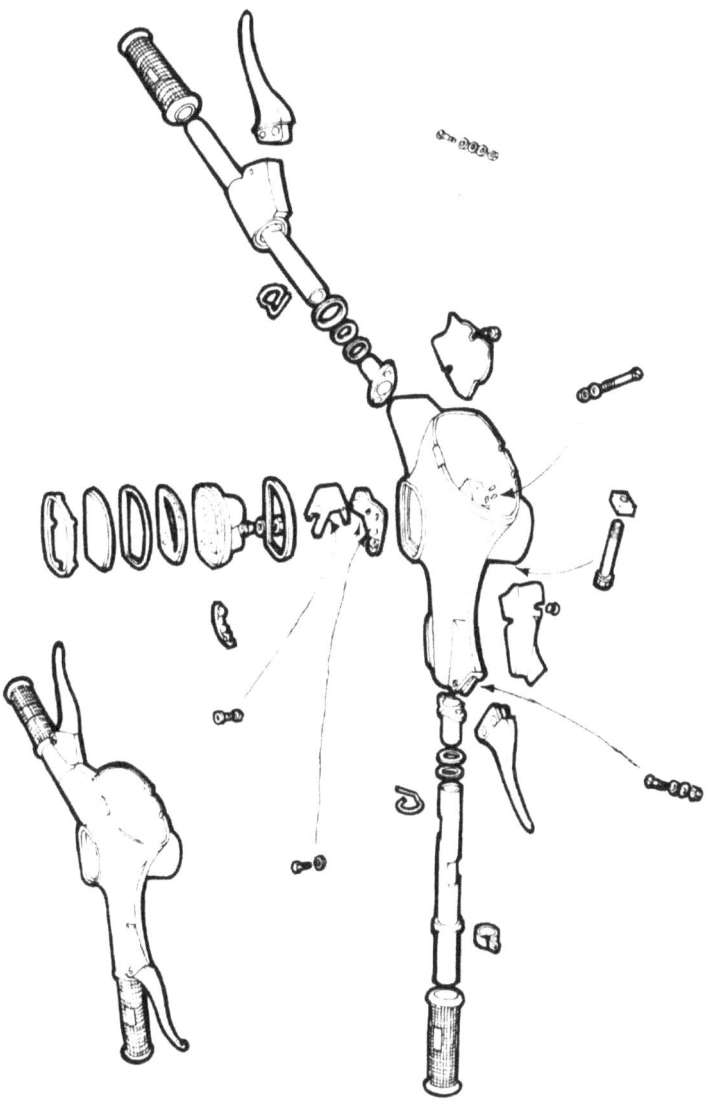

Fig. 28. Vespa 125/150 Controls "exploded"

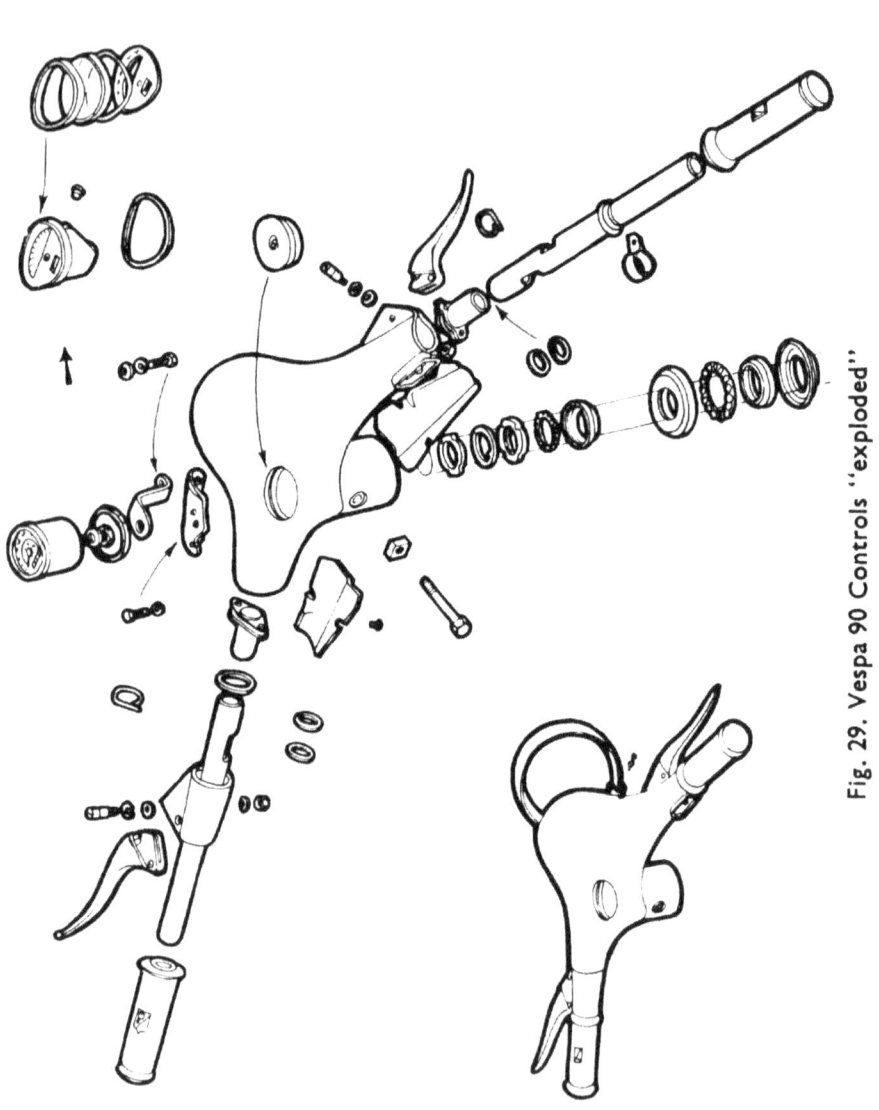

Fig. 29. Vespa 90 Controls "exploded"

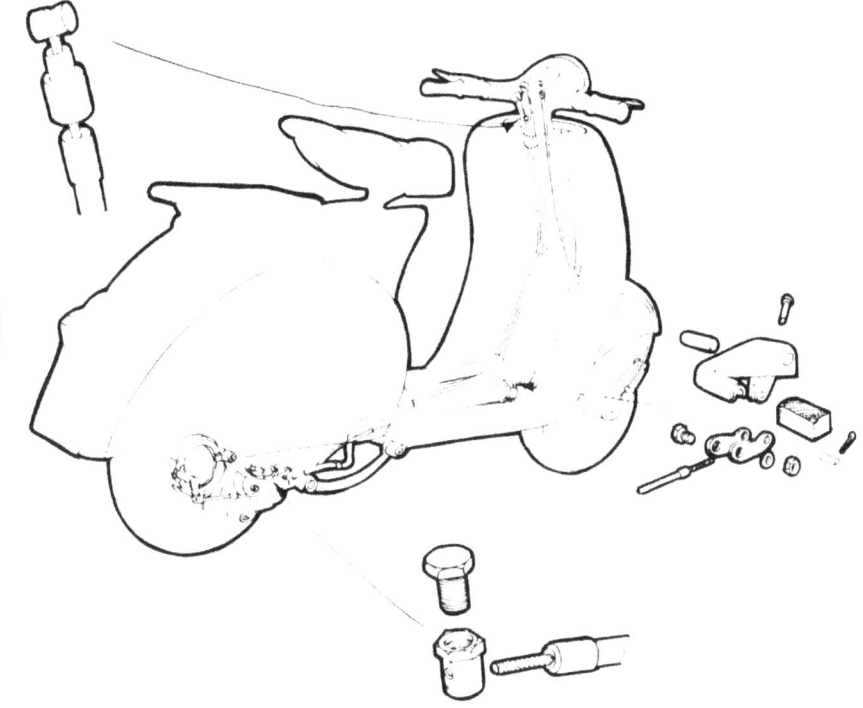

Fig. 30. Control Cable Layout, Vespa 125/150. The manner in which the cables are run through frame conduits is typical Vespa practice

outer in place. As breaks are likelier to occur near the control itself, rather than the component, this usually means withdrawing the inner cable from the far end. Once this has been done, the replacement cable should be oiled, and fed carefully into the outer casing from the control end. Once it is through, the control nipple can be engaged and the cable connected to its unit and adjusted in the normal way.

Where the outer casing itself is damaged it is possible to fit a new one without dismantling, providing the following sequence is adopted. First, obtain a length of copper wire a few inches over twice the length of the replacement casing. Pass this wire through the new casing and form a "head" at the top end so that it cannot be pulled through. Feed the lower "free" end through the old casing, so that the lower end of the new casing butts hard against the upper end of the old. By pulling on the free end of the copper wire, the new casing will press the old one out of position and will be drawn through the frame and into place, ready to accept the new inner cable.

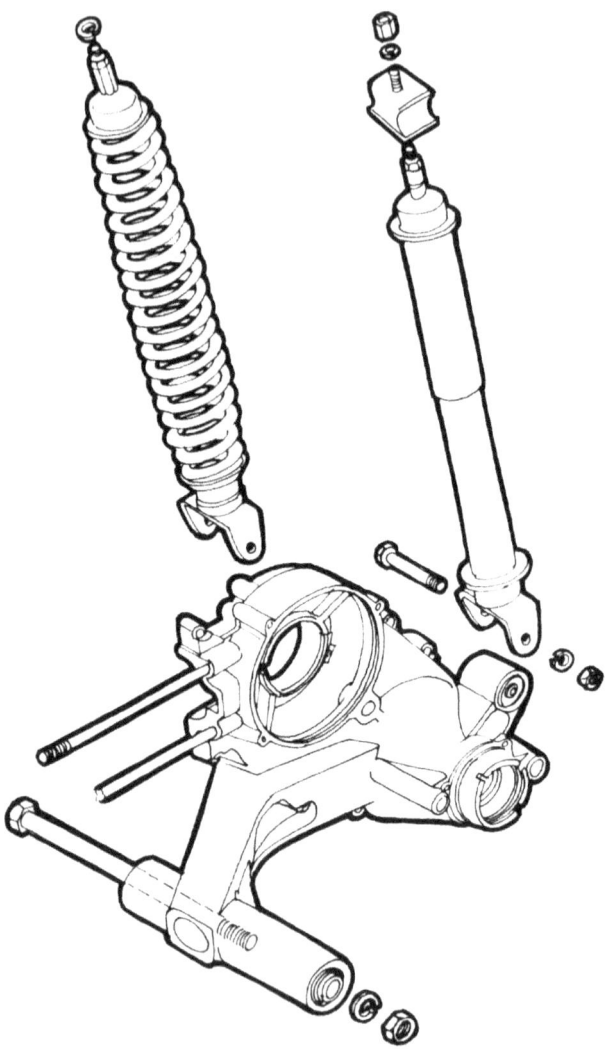

Fig. 31. Vespa Rear Spring and Damper Attachment

Rear Brake Cable. On the foot brake, the cable ends in a trunnion through which is passed a pin. This, in turn, is locked with a split pin. Undo the split pin to free the trunnion.

The pedal itself is similarly held by a pin passing through its pivot. This pin is exposed when the brake pedal is depressed.

Centre Stand

According to the model, this is held either by two 10 mm-headed bolts passing upwards through the stand brackets, or by two bolts passed through the footboards into the brackets. The stand spring is hooked into position between the stand and the frame, the longer hook facing to the front.

10 On the road

LET's not run away with the idea that all one can do with a scooter is maintain it! Life would be pretty dull if that were so. The primary object of the machine is to be ridden—and that is an art in itself.

True enough, almost anybody can step aboard a Vespa and make some sort of effort at riding it. But nowadays the roads are crowded, and it is not enough that you can simply stay aboard. You have to be able to handle the machine properly if you are not to be a menace to other road-users—and, of course, to yourself.

Before you even *think* of riding, buy yourself a safety helmet and make a rule never to go out on two wheels—even if it's only down to the disco—unless you have it on. To be safety-conscious doesn't mean you're soft—it simply shows that there's something inside your head worth preserving. Moreover, most of the year (in Britain, at any rate) you *need* good head protection from the weather alone—and a safety helmet is the best.

You'll need either goggles or a visor, too. You may think that if the machine has a screen you can get by without. So you can, as far as rain is concerned. Airborne grit and insects, however, can still get through to your eyes—and the impact of a wasp on an eyeball is very far from pleasant. At a pinch, a pair of sun-glasses will suffice—but I *have* had a wasp end up impaled half-way over the frames. Another half-inch and I'd have been regretting not bothering to put my goggles on.

If you have never ridden a scooter before, the best possible way to learn how to do it is to enrol in the RAC/A-CU Learner Training Scheme. Run by the clubs in many parts of the country, this is a course of lectures and practical riding lessons that should take you to a standard above that needed to pass the MoT Driving Test. All instruction is on private ground until you are judged to be capable of taking the machine on to the roads, and at the end of it all you receive a proficiency certificate. Details can be obtained from the Manager of the RAC Motorcycle Department at 85 Pall Mall, London, SW1. If there is a course in your area, he will tell you how to enrol. Costs are moderate—far, far less than an L-driver has to pay for lessons from a commercial school—and the grounding you will get is worth ten times the outlay.

If there is no course, and you are a raw beginner, then you'll have to rely upon self-tuition. That means forming your own riding habits—and if they are good ones they will save you quite a bit of money. Bad habits lead to wrecked bikes—and wrecked bikes mean money down the drain.

Start your studies in an armchair, learning all about your machine and its controls. Having memorized the location of each of them (don't forget that the switches for the "electrics" and selecting the "reserve" position for the fuel are controls as well) close your eyes and pretend you are on the machine. Then give yourself a series of quick tests—"Apply the front brake," "Dip the lights," "Change into top," for example—and at the same time make the appropriate hand movements.

The idea is to accustom yourself to operating the controls quickly and *without* having to look at them. When you're on the road, the place to be looking is at what's ahead of you. And if you think that speed of control operation is a purist's quibble, just remember that even 30 mph represents 44 feet covered each second. Lose only half a second groping for the brakes and you have covered virtually two car lengths—and that could well be the margin between a safe stop and a serious accident.

When you're satisfied with the progress of your dummy runs, put the Vespa on its stand, sit on it, and go through the entire exercise again. This time, actually operate the controls—*again, with your eyes shut*—and check the results each time. When you are absolutely sure that you can find and use each control instinctively, it's time to start the roadwork.

Before you do, though, make sure you have complied with all the legal requirements. You must have your driving licence, and the licence *must* be signed. Either a Certificate of Insurance or a cover note to prove you are indemnified against third-party risks is vital. It is not only a serious offence to ride without cover—it is also stupid, and a short cut to bankruptcy if you should happen to injure somebody.

If your machine is over three years old (legally speaking, that means three years from the original date of registration) it must have an MoT Test Certificate. And as a learner rider, you can only use the machine on the road if it carries regulation-sized L-plates at front and rear. The tax disc must be up to date, and properly displayed at the front left-hand side of the machine. And if you carry a pillion passenger—not advisable in any event until you have some experience under your belt—that passenger must be the holder of a full licence.

Right now! Obviously enough, the first step is to start the engine. Then you need to know how to control it. You'll already have practised turning the right-hand twist-grip backwards and forwards of course, but what matters is knowing exactly how the engine responds.

With the scooter on its stand, check that it is in neutral. Then switch on the fuel and, if it's a chilly day, operate the strangler. Where appropriate, switch on the ignition. Have the twist-grip slightly towards you—about an eighth of a turn open—and operate the kickstarter. There's a trick to this, though. You *don't* actually kick it. The idea is to apply a constant pressure all the way through, not just to jab it. That way, you really spin the engine over and get a series of good sparks—something that is impossible with just a dab on the pedal. Most Vespas will start first kick.

With the engine running, spend a few minutes (no more, or you'll make yourself highly unpopular with the neighbours!) gently opening and closing the throttle. Again, don't jerk it. Roll it smoothly towards you to speed the engine up, and away from you to slow it. "Gently," by the way, does *not* mean "slowly." All control movements should be incisive, but smooth. You'll soon find that the engine is responsive to the least movement of your right hand, and that by holding steady at any point the engine note steadies too. But remember, during this familiarization period, that the unit is not under load, and that consequently it will speed up fast as you twist the grip open. So don't overdo it, or the result will be a sudden blast of sound that will have you snapping the throttle shut in sheer panic! The range between tick-over and one-third throttle should be about right for your practice session.

Smooth throttle control will mean smooth riding later on, so if you're not satisfied with the results try this exercise again until you are sure you have the "feel" of it. You are then ready for your first excursion.

One doesn't always have much of a choice in these matters, but if you can possibly arrange it do try to take your first steps on a quiet road or—at the very least—at a quiet time of day so far as other traffic is concerned. If you're a countryman, of course, the ideal scheme is to ask a local farmer to let you use a corner of a field or a stretch of farm road. Even in towns you can often make use of a car park on a Sunday morning.

The first hurdle is to learn how to get a smooth take-off. This involves a neat co-ordination of throttle and clutch, together with a balancing act. But really it's quite easy—especially the balancing. The trick, there, is to get your feet off the ground and on to the footboard *as soon as possible* when the machine starts to move. Till then you are unbalanced. Riders who trail their feet are bad riders, and are only making things far more difficult for themselves into the bargain. The aim should be, eventually, to get your feet aboard as soon as the clutch bites and the machine starts to move forward. For a start, though, just ensure that both feet are firmly on the machine by the time the clutch is fully home.

Before you actually set off on your ride, however, have yet another short practice session at a standstill to get the "feel" of the clutch. Roll the machine off the stand and start the engine—or vice versa if you prefer—and then pull out the clutch and engage first gear with the machine standing on its wheels and with your legs straddling it. If you can't stretch enough to get both feet on the ground, keep your left foot down and well forward, have your right foot on the footboard, and keep the model tilted to the left.

Now release the clutch lever—gently, and not too fast—until you feel that the clutch is beginning to engage. The engine will begin to slow down, and you will feel the machine beginning to edge forward. Immediately whip out the clutch and repeat the exercise two or three times more. You will soon find that the lever can be released quite quickly to the point of initial engagement—where the clutch plates are just beginning to transmit

ON THE ROAD 69

Fig. 32. This is what happens if you let the clutch out too fast! The front wheel lifts, and the machine jumps forward before the engine stalls

drive—and can be checked accurately there. This is the point at which, on moving off, you start to give a little more throttle.

As soon as you are sure you can control the clutch accurately over this vital initial movement you are ready for your run. This time, as you check the movement of the clutch lever, open the throttle a little more—just how much will depend on your particular machine, but about an eighth to a quarter of a turn should be about right. The scooter will move away, still with the clutch slipping. Get your feet on to the boards at once, and let the clutch fully home as soon as you have covered a couple of yards. Now control the speed on the throttle alone, remembering to move it smoothly. Rolling it back towards you will speed the machine up. Twisting it away from you will slow it down. Practise controlling the speed with the twistgrip until it is time to stop. Then—in one movement—close the grip, pull the clutch lever fully out and apply the rear brake lightly. As the machine comes to rest, drop your left foot to support it, select neutral, and release the clutch.

This initial self-training may not sound like sampling the joys of the open road—but the road will still be there tomorrow, and the day after. Get your groundwork done properly first, and you will be able to tackle real riding without anxiety later on.

Fig. 33. Why you should always use both brakes for stopping. As this picture shows, under deceleration the weight shifts forward and the front wheel gains adhesion. The rear wheel becomes lightly loaded—note the small contact area between the rear tyre and the road. Using the rear brake alone causes skidding

Once you have become thoroughly used to starting and stopping in this way, move on to the next stage, which is to make your stop using *both* brakes instead of the rear brake only. You will soon find that you can apply the front brake with your fingers while operating the twist grip with the heel of the hand. After that, try stopping on the front brake alone—caressing, rather than pressing, the lever in the early stages until you have the reaction weighed up.

Gear changing comes next. After moving off, accelerate up to about 10 mph in first. Then—all in one co-ordinated movement—snap the throttle shut, pull out the clutch, select second gear, drop the clutch again, and give about quarter-throttle. It sounds a lot, but you'll soon acquire the knack. Changing down into bottom again demands exactly the same technique save for one vital difference. Instead of the throttle being closed as the clutch and gears are operated, it is either left open or else is "blipped" —i.e. snapped open and shut—as the change is made. The idea is to speed up the engine to the higher revs needed in the lower gear, so getting a clean gear engagement.

From this exercise, it is a logical step to go on to the engagement and disengagement of third gear and, on four-speeders, top gear. Within a few hours, you should have mastered the knack of moving off, going up and down through the gearbox, and stopping smoothly. With the Vespa, one further refinement is possible once your throttle control action is accurate. You can make all gear changes on the move simply by turning the left-hand twist-grip and without operating the clutch at all.

So far, all our exercises have been in straight-line motoring. But roads are not all straight—you have to turn some time! And turns on a scooter are made simply by leaning the machine in the direction you want to go—*not* by turning the handlebars.

Strictly speaking, there is only one correct angle of bank for any given radius of turn at any given speed. Don't let that worry you—the steering set-up of a scooter is so designed that the machine will look after that aspect most of the time. What the rider has to do is to develop an innate sense of speed, balance and position on the road so that each corner is approached at the right speed, in the right gear and on the right line. Only experience will produce the sixth sense that enables this equation to be set up on each and every occasion. In the formative stages, just remember that it is better to approach a corner relatively slowly and then accelerate through it than to come in fast and have to jam on the brakes and perhaps overshoot. Generally speaking, third gear and a moderate angle of bank will take you through.

Emergency stops should be practised occasionally once you have gained in proficiency. The important point here is to get both brakes on as fast as you can, yet to avoid skidding. If the wheels lock up, it will add several feet at least to your overall stopping distance. Give the front brake a slight "lead" over the rear, since the back end tends to lose adhesion and the front to gain it under sharp deceleration. With brakes in good condition, it should be possible to come to a dead stop in about 32 feet from the moment that the controls are operated. But there's the "thinking distance" to take into account as well. Even a top racing driver takes a quarter of a second to react before he starts applying the brakes—and at 30 mph that means 11 feet between spotting the danger and beginning to take action. Most of us have far slower reactions—around three-quarters of a second is average. And that effectively *doubles* the braking distance. So it pays to think ahead and to take precautions against what may happen a few seconds later.

Riding on wet roads calls for extra care simply because the friction between the tyres and the road is reduced—which means you have less grip. Correcting a skid on a greasy surface calls for immediate action if the scooter is to stay upright. Leave the brakes and throttle alone, and steer into the skid. If the machine is sliding to the left, put your weight to the left and centralize the handlebars. If it is sliding to the right, put your weight to the right and, again, centralize the bars. The reaction is, in fact, instinctive. But braking will only make matters worse by locking the wheels —and, unfortunately, braking is an instinctive reaction too.

It is easier to avoid skidding than to get out of it. As a rule, skids will only develop if the machine is changing speed or changing direction. Avoidance, then, demands the fewest possible changes of speed or direction under slippery conditions—and the gentlest possible handling of the controls when such changes *are* made. On corners, keep the angle of bank down to the minimum required to get round on line. On straights, accelerate gently and brake gently. In traffic, leave ample clear road between yourself and the vehicle in front, so that if he stops suddenly you can pull up without having to try an emergency stop. And if some inconsiderate fool barges into your braking space—well, drop back. You may prove a point by running into his back bumper, but it's an uncomfortable way of winning an argument!

When the roads are covered with ice and snow, the place for your scooter is in its garage—at least until you are an experienced rider. Not that snow, in itself, is particularly tricky. Virgin snow is actually a rather pleasant surface on which to ride. Snow that has been churned and rutted by other vehicles is a somewhat different matter, especially if it has subsequently frozen over. And ice—particularly near-invisible black ice—is downright treacherous. The first you know of it is that suddenly there is no tyre hum. Next thing, the machine is sideways-on to the road and virtually out of control. Even experts can come a cropper under those conditions, so don't chance your arm.

If you *must* go out, the technique to employ is to treat the throttle as if it was made of bone china and the brake controls as if they were wired to a time bomb! Every action must be smooth and unhurried. Keep the machine as upright as you can, taking corners more by leaning the body weight the way you want to go, but without banking the machine more than a few degrees. This applies pressure to the bars automatically, providing your balance is right.

The classic advice is to use the highest possible gear at the lowest possible speed, and to keep close to the kerb to obtain the benefit of any grit accumulating near the gutters. Both techniques may well be right, but in the twenty-six years or so since I started riding I have developed my own views on that!

My method of dealing with snow-bound roads—traffic permitting, of course—is to keep as close to the crown as possible to gain the advantage of minimum road camber and to allow myself the maximum amount of road space for recovery should the machine start to slide. In my view, the further away one keeps from that potentially lethal kerbstone the better. If the machine *does* start to go, it is usually possible to hold it against the camber and keep it upright, slithering the wheels safely if inelegantly into the gutter in a controlled slide rather than an uncontrolled skid.

Also, I use the lowest gear that will give me the range of speeds that appears appropriate to the conditions. This gives better throttle control and reduces (often even eliminates) transmission snatch. But be warned —this technique demands really smooth and disciplined throttle control. And it also demands concentration, since a sudden jolt might otherwise cause you to give the grip an involuntary tweak—with disastrous results.

It is up to you to choose your method. The classic style has worked for millions of riders over the years—and my style has worked for me. Whichever you use, remember that the whole object of the journey is to arrive in one piece, so don't get impatient.

Appendix 1
Data

	V9A1	V9SS1	VMA1	VMA2	VLB1	VBC1
Bore (mm)	47	47	55	55	57	57
Stroke (mm)	51	51	51	51	57	57
Capacity (c.c.)	88·5	88·5	121·17	121·17	145·45	145·45
Compression ratio	7·2	8·7	7·2	7·2	7·5	7·4
Main Jet	63	82	82/110	74/100	102	88
Start	50	50	50/100	50/100	60	60
Pilot	38	38	38/100	42/100	42	42
Slide	—	—	2	2	—	—
Carburettor	SHB 16/16	SHB 16/16	SHB 16/16	SHB 16/16	SI 20/170	SI 20/15D
Oil recommendation	SAE 30	SAE 30	SAE 30	SAE 30	SAE 30	SAE 30
Tank capacity/petroil ratio	1·15 gal/50:1	1·15 gal/50:1	1·23 gal/50:1	1·23 gal/50:1	1·7 gal/50:1	1·7 gal/50:1
Gearbox oil recommendation	SAE 30 or 20/W 30	SAE 30 or 20/W 30	SAE 30 or 20/W 30	SAE 30	SAE 30	SAE 30
Plug recommendation	KLG F80 Champion L81	KLG F70 or F75 Champion L81	KLG F70 or F75 Champion L86 or L7	KLG F70 or F75 Champion L86 or L7	KLG F70 or F75 Champion L86 or L7	KLG F70 or F75 Champion L86 or L7
Plug gap	0·020 in.	0·020 in.	0·025 in.	0·025 in.	0·025 in.	0·025 in.
Contact-breaker gap	0·015 in.	0·015 in.	0·015 in.	0·015 in.	0·015 in.	0·015 in.
Timing	19° ±1° BTDC	19° ±1° BTDC	25° ±1° BTDC	25° ±1° BTDC	22° ±1° BTDC	22° ±1° BTDC

Data (contd.)

	V9A1	V9SS1	VMA1	VMA2	VLB1	VBC1
Tyre pressures:						
Front	17 psi	17 psi	17 psi	17 psi	16—17 psi	16 psi
Rear	23 psi	23 psi	23 psi	23 psi	25 psi	19 psi
	(33 pillion)	(33 pillion)	(33 pillion)	(33 pillion)	(35 pillion)	(33 pillion)
Tyre sizes	3·00 × 10	3·00 × 10	3·00 × 10	3·00 × 10	3·50 × 10	3·50 × 8
Bulbs:						
Headlamp	6 V 25/25 W	6 V 25/25 W	6 V 25/25 W	6 V 25/25 W	6 V 25/25 W	6 V 25/25 W
Tail	6 V 5 W	6 V 5 W	6 V 5 W	6 V 5 W	6 V 5 W	6 V 5 W
Stop	6 V 10 W	6 V 10 W	6 V 10 W	6 V 10 W	6 V 10 W	6 V 10 W
Park	6 V 5 W	6 V 5 W	6 V 5 W	6 V 5 W	6 V 5 W	6 V 5 W
Speedo	—	—	6 V 0·06 W	6 V 0·06 W	6 V 0·06 W	6 V 0·06 W

Appendix 2
Roadside troubles

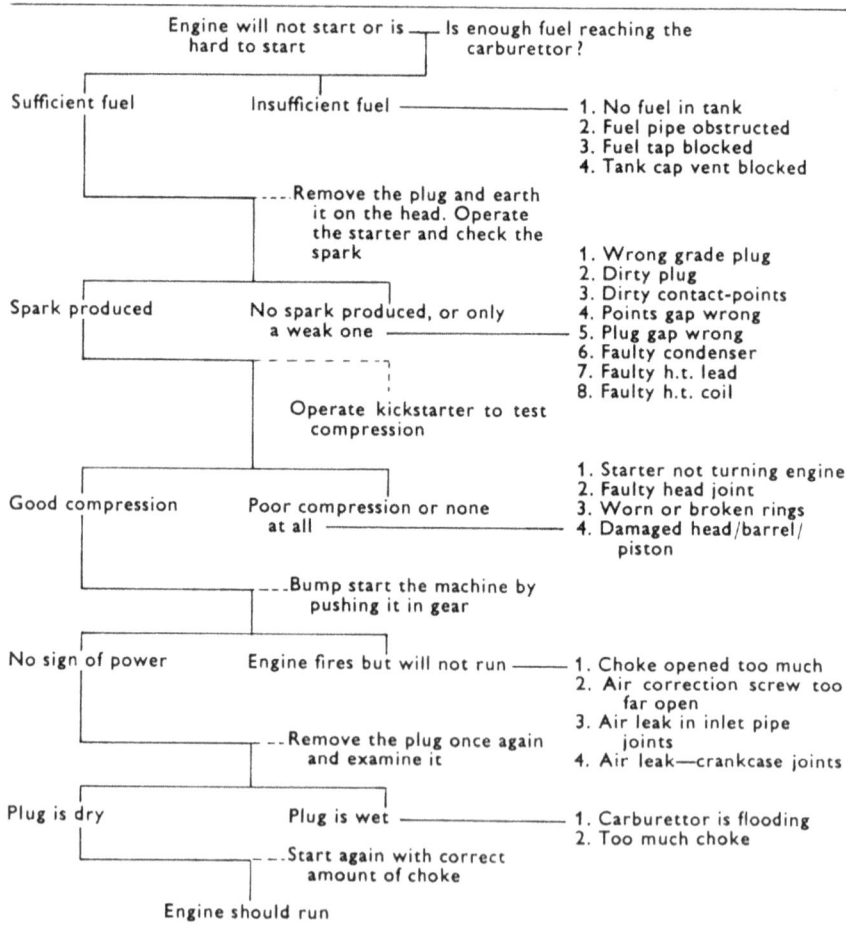

Running	Fault Check	Possible Trouble
	Lack of speed or pulling power — — — — Lift and spin both wheels	
Both turn easily	Either does not turn easily	1. Brake is binding 2. Damaged wheel bearing 3. Hub needs greasing
	— — —Check the tyres with a pressure gauge	
Tyre pressures are correct	Tyre pressures are wrong	1. Punctured tyre 2. Faulty valve 3. Neglected maintenance
	— — —Engage first gear, apply the brakes and rev. the engine	
Engine stalls	Engine still keeps running	1. Clutch is slipping— adjustment wrong 2. Clutch plates are worn
	— — —Slightly rev. the engine in neutral	
Engine speeds up	Engine does not speed up	1. Choke is closed 2. Air cleaner is clogged 3. Fuel line is clogged 4. Fuel cap vent blocked 5. Silencer is clogged 6. Main jet obstructed 7. Air leak in inlet pipe 8. Petroil ratio wrong
	— — —Test the machine on good roads. Then check the ignition timing and points gap	
Timing/gap correct	Timing/gap wrong	1. Defective adjustment
	— — —Operate the kickstarter and test the compression	
Good compression	No compression	1. Rings and/or bore worn 2. Leaking joints
	— — —Strip and examine the carburettor	
Carburettor is not dirty	Carburettor is dirty	1. Dirt is blocking jets
	— — —Remove and examine the sparking plug	
Plug is clean and not discoloured	Plug is dirty or discoloured	1. Plug not properly cleaned 2. Plug is of the wrong grade
	— — —Does the engine overheat?	
Engine does not overheat	Engine overheats	1. Excess carbon in the combustion chamber 2. Petrol of too low an octane rating 3. Clutch slips 4. Mixture is too weak 5. Petroil ratio wrong
	— — —Test under high-speed acceleration	
Engine does not "pink" or knock Power should now be restored	Engine does pink or knock	1. Petrol is of too low an octane rating 2. Piston, rings, and/or bore badly worn

APPENDIX 2

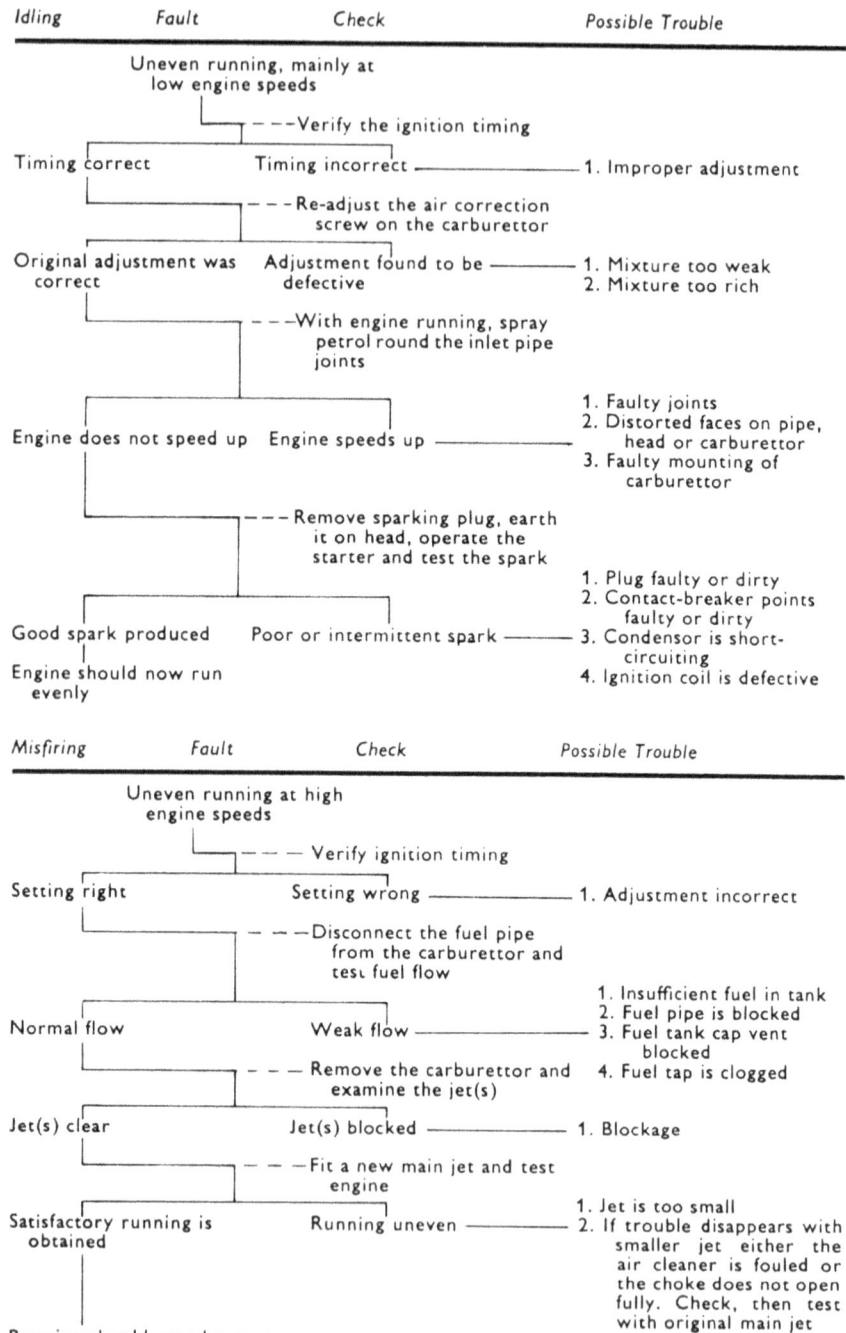

Smoke	Fault	Check	Possible Cause
	Excessive smoke from the exhaust — — — Run at continuous high engine revs.		1. Worn piston, rings, bore 2. Too much oil in fuel 3. Rings fitted inverted
Normal smoke level results | No problem		Coloured smoke produced ———	4. Damage to piston or bore 5. Faulty crankcase seats 6. Residual oil in silencer due to fuel being left on

Clutch	Fault	Check	Possible Cause
	Apparent power loss ├ — — - Adjustment of clutch | Clutch slips —————— ├ — — - Operate the clutch and engage gear at low speed | Engine stalls ——————		1. Weakened springs 2. Worn or distorted clutch plates 3. Worn or distorted friction linings 1. Plates or friction discs distorted 2. Clutch springs of uneven strength

Gears	Fault	Check	Possible Cause
	Impossible to change gear └──┐ - - -Clutch operation Clutch operates perfectly ——— | Faulty selection or jumps — out of gear		1. Gear-change cable broken 2. Gear-change cable adjustment wrong 3. Gear-change selector defective 1. Dogs on gears worn 2. Selector bent or worn 3. Gear-change cables faulty or wrongly adjusted

Noises	Fault	Check	Possible Cause
	Tinkling from region of ——— Plug —————		1. Wrong plug 2. Faulty plug
	Metallic knock or ringing —— Internals ——— from cylinder		1. Worn piston, rings, bore 2. Worn small-end bearing 3. "Pinking," caused by excess carbon in the head
	Rattle from clutch side of —— Clutch ————— engine		1. Clutch drum slots worn, allowing plates to move 2. Clutch loose on its splines
	Rumble from engine ————— Crankshaft ——		1. Excessive end float 2. Worn or damaged main bearings

APPENDIX 2

Steering		Check	Possible Cause
		Tyre pressures	1. Too hard 2. Too soft 3. Not adjusted for pillion passenger
Machine tends to skid or pull either way		Operation of handlebars	1. Head bearings too tight 2. Steering race balls damaged 3. Stem is bent
		Vibration from front or rear wheels	1. Wheel bearings worn 2. Dented wheel rims 3. Rear fork pivot and/or bushing loose or worn 4. Badly bent 5. Faulty tyre
Machine tends to skid or to pull one side only			1. Unbalanced dampers 2. Wheels out of line 3. Front fork bent 4. Body distorted 5. Front spindle bent 6. Loose head bearing

Springing	Fault	Check	Possible Cause
		Tyre pressures	1. Too hard 2. Too soft 3. Not adjusted for pillion passenger
	Unsatisfactory operation of suspension	Too hard	1. Front or rear damper not operating
		Too soft	1. Weakened spring 2. Load is too great
	Noisy operation		1. Friction between the fixed and moving parts of the damper 2. Friction between the casing and the spring 3. Hydraulic fluid level incorrect at front or rear due to leakage

Braking	Fault	Check	Possible Cause
	Brakes lack power	Adjustment at front and rear	1. Front or rear brake cable binds 2. Contact between shoe and drum defective 3. Water in the drums 4. Oil or grease on the linings
	No adjustment possible		1. Linings are worn 2. Operating cam worn 3. Shoe worn at point of contact with cam
	Noisy operation		1. Wear on linings 2. Dirt on the linings 3. Lining faces rough 4. Operating-arm bush worn

Index

AIR cleaner, 125/150, 40
 filter, cleaning, 40

BATTERY—
 specific gravity, 47
 topping-up, 47
Brake, front—
 Vespa 90, exploded, 57
 Vespa 125/150, exploded, 58
Brakes—
 front, dismantling, 55
 operation of, 70
 shoes, refitting, 55
 shoes, removal, 55
Bulbs, checking, 50
 types, 76

CABLES, layout, 63
Carburettor—
 jet sizes, 75
 reassembly, 40
 removal, 38
 slides, sizes, 75
 stripping, 39
 Vespa 90, exploded, 38
 Vespa 125/150, exploded, 39
Central stand, removal, 65
Clutch, operation, 68
 stripping, 34
Contact-breaker points—
 gap, 75
 installing, 44
 refacing, 47
 removal, 44
 setting, 43
 worn, 44
Control cables, renewal, 60
Controls—
 Vespa 90, exploded, 62
 Vespa 125/150, exploded, 61

DAMPER, Vespa 125/150, 59
 rear, 64
Driving licence, 67

ELECTRICS, layout—
 Vespa 90, 48
 Vespa 125/150, 49
Engine—
 operation, 4
 reassembly, 36
 removal, 13, 28
 stripping, 29
 swivelling, for decoke, 28
 Vespa 125/150, exploded, 29
Engine-transmission unit—
 Vespa 90, 6
 Vespa 125/150, 7

FORK link—
 bearings, removal, 60
 removal, 59
Front fork—
 removal, 56
 Vespa 90, exploded, 57
 Vespa 125/150, exploded, 58
Fuel consumption, excessive, 27
 tap, 41

GEAR cluster, assembly sequence, 37
Gearbox—
 reassembly, 37
 stripping, 34
 Vespa 90, exploded, 35
 Vespa 125/150, exploded, 31
Gears, operation, 70

HYDROMETER, using, 50

IDLING speed, adjustment, 40
Insurance, 67

JETS—
  removal, 39
  sizes, 75

LEARNING to ride, 66

MoT Test Certificate, 67
Magneto—
  stripping, 34
  Vespa, 90, 45
  Vespa 125/150, 46
Maintenance, routine, 19, 20

NOISES, 26

OILS—
  engine, recommended, 75
  gearbox, recommended, 75

PETROIL, ratios, 75
Primary drive—
  Vespa 90, exploded, 33
  Vespa 125/150, exploded, 32
Power, loss of, 26

RAC/A-CU Training Scheme, 66
Rear brake cable, trunnion, 65
Riding kit, 66

SNOW, riding in, 72
Sparking plugs, recommended, 75

Spring—
  front, Vespa 125/150, 59
  rear, 64
Stand, spring, fitting, 65
Starting, difficult, 25, 26
Steering head—
  bearing, 56
  bearing, adjustment, 56
  bearing, removal, 59, 60
Suspension, bottoming, 27

TEST lamp, using, 43
Throttle, operation, 68
Timing—
  adjustment, diagram, 43
  checking, 42
  re-setting, 44
  settings, 75
Top Dead Centre, determining, 43
Trouble tracing, 77
Tyres—
  pressures, 76
  sizes, 76

VIBRATION, 26

WIRING diagram, visual—
  Vespa 90, 52
  Vespa 90S, 51
  Vespa 125, 53
  Vespa 150, 54

ARE YOU:
INTERESTED IN EUROPEAN, IMPORT & EXOTIC AUTOMOBILES?

DO YOU:
DO YOUR OWN MAINTENANCE?

If you answered yes to either of these questions, then you should check out our automobile books and manuals. We have included a sample listing of some of our featured marques. However, for complete details and the most up-to-date information, please visit our website.

— www.VelocePress.com —

The fastest growing specialist USA publisher of niche market automotive books and manuals.

All VelocePress titles are available through your local independent bookseller, Amazon.com or direct from VelocePress. Wholesale customers may also purchase direct or from the Ingram Book Group.

AUTOBOOKS WORKSHOP MANUALS

ALFA ROMEO GIULIA 1300, 1600, 1750, 2000 1962-1978 WSM
AUSTIN HEALEY SPRITE, MG MIDGET 1958-1980 WSM
BMW 1600 1966-1973 WSM
BMW 2000 & 2002 1966-1976 WSM
BMW 2500, 2800, 3.0 & 3.3 1968-1977 WSM
BMW 316, 320, 320i 1975-1977 WSM
BMW 518, 520, 520i 1973-1981 WSM
FIAT 1100, 1100D, 1100R & 1200 1957-1969 WSM
FIAT 124 1966-1974 WSM
FIAT 124 SPORT 1966-1975 WSM
FIAT 125 & 125 SPECIAL 1967-1973 WSM
FIAT 126, 126L, 126 DV, 126/650 & 126/650 DV 1972-1982 WSM
FIAT 127 SALOON, SPECIAL & SPORT, 900, 1050 1971-1981 WSM
FIAT 128 1969-1982 WSM
FIAT 1300, 1500 1961-1967 WSM
FIAT 131 MIRAFIORI 1975-1982 WSM
FIAT 132 1972-1982 WSM
FIAT 500 1957-1973 WSM
FIAT 600, 600D & MULTIPLA 1955-1969 WSM
FIAT 850 1964-1972 WSM
JAGUAR E-TYPE 1961-1972 WSM
JAGUAR MK 1, 2 1955-1969 WSM
JAGUAR S TYPE, 420 1963-1968 WSM
JAGUAR XK 120, 140, 150 MK 7, 8, 9 1948-1961 WSM
LAND ROVER 1, 2 1948-1961 WSM
MERCEDES-BENZ 190 1959-1968 WSM
MERCEDES-BENZ 220/8 1968-1972 WSM
MERCEDES-BENZ 220B 1959-1965 WSM
MERCEDES-BENZ 230 1963-1968 WSM
MERCEDES-BENZ 250 1968-1972 WSM
MERCEDES-BENZ 280 1968-1972 WSM
MG MIDGET TA-TF 1936-1955 WSM
MINI 1959-1980 WSM
MORRIS MINOR 1952-1971 WSM
PEUGEOT 404 1960-1975 WSM
PORSCHE 911 1964-1973 WSM
PORSCHE 911 1970-1977 WSM
RENAULT 16 1965-1979 WSM
RENAULT 8, 10, 1100 1962-1971 WSM
ROVER 3500, 3500S 1968-1976 WSM
SUNBEAM RAPIER, ALPINE 1955-1965 WSM
TRIUMPH SPITFIRE, GT6, VITESSE 1962-1968 WSM
TRIUMPH TR2, TR3, TR3A 1952-1962 WSM
TRIUMPH TR4, TR4A 1961-1967 WSM
VOLKSWAGEN BEETLE 1968-1977 WSM

BROOKLANDS BOOKS & ROAD TEST PORTFOLIOS (RTP)

AC CARS 1904-2009
ALFA ROMEO 1920-1933 ROAD TEST PORTFOLIO
ALFA ROMEO 1934-1940 ROAD TEST PORTFOLIO
BRABHAM RALT HONDA THE RON TAURANAC STORY
BUGATTI TYPE 10 TO TYPE 40 ROAD TEST PORTFOLIO
BUGATTI TYPE 10 TO TYPE 251 ROAD TEST PORTFOLIO
BUGATTI TYPE 41 TO TYPE 55 ROAD TEST PORTFOLIO
BUGATTI TYPE 57 TO TYPE 251 ROAD TEST PORTFOLIO
DELAHAYE ROAD TEST PORTFOLIO
FERRARI ROAD CARS 1946-1956 ROAD TEST PORTFOLIO
FIAT 500 1936-1972 ROAD TEST PORTFOLIO
FIAT DINO ROAD TEST PORTFOLIO
HISPANO SUIZA ROAD TEST PORTFOLIO
HONDA ST1100/ST1300 PAN EUROPEAN 1990-2002 RTP
JAGUAR MK1 & MK2 ROAD TEST PORTFOLIO
LOTUS CORTINA ROAD TEST PORTFOLIO
MV AGUSTA F4 750 & 1000 1997-2007 ROAD TEST PORTFOLIO
TATRA CARS ROAD TEST PORTFOLIO

VELOCEPRESS AUTOMOBILE BOOKS & MANUALS

ABARTH BUYERS GUIDE
AUSTIN-HEALEY 6-CYLINDER WSM
BMW 600 LIMOUSINE FACTORY WSM
BMW 600 LIMOUSINE OWNERS HAND BOOK & SERVICE MANUAL
BMW ISETTA FACTORY WSM
BOOK OF THE CARRERA PANAMERICANA - MEXICAN ROAD RACE
COMPLETE CATALOG OF JAPANESE MOTOR VEHICLES
DIALED IN - THE JAN OPPERMAN STORY
FERRARI 250/GT SERVICE AND MAINTENANCE
FERRARI 308 SERIES BUYER'S AND OWNER'S GUIDE
FERRARI BERLINETTA LUSSO
FERRARI BROCHURES AND SALES LITERATURE 1946-1967
FERRARI BROCHURES AND SALES LITERATURE 1968-1989
FERRARI GUIDE TO PERFORMANCE
FERRARI OPP, MAINTENANCE & SERVICE H/BOOKS 1948-1963
FERRARI OWNER'S HANDBOOK
FERRARI SERIAL NUMBERS PART I - ODD NUMBERS TO 21399
FERRARI SERIAL NUMBERS PART II - EVEN NUMBERS TO 1050
FERRARI SPYDER CALIFORNIA
FERRARI TUNING TIPS & MAINTENANCE TECHNIQUES
HENRY'S FABULOUS MODEL "A" FORD
HOW TO BUILD A FIBERGLASS CAR
HOW TO BUILD A RACING CAR
HOW TO RESTORE THE MODEL 'A' FORD
IF HEMINGWAY HAD WRITTEN A RACING NOVEL
JAGUAR E-TYPE 3.8 & 4.2 WSM
LE MANS 24 (THE BOOK THAT THE FILM WAS BASED ON)
MASERATI BROCHURES AND SALES LITERATURE
MASERATI OWNER'S HANDBOOK
METROPOLITAN FACTORY WSM
MGA & MGB OWNERS HANDBOOK & WSM
OBERT'S FIAT GUIDE
PERFORMANCE TUNING THE SUNBEAM TIGER
PORSCHE 356 1948-1965 WSM
PORSCHE 912 WSM
SOUPING THE VOLKSWAGEN
TRIUMPH TR2, TR3, TR4 1953-1965 WSM
VEDA ORR'S NEW REVISED HOT ROD PICTORIAL
VOLKSWAGEN TRANSPORTER, TRUCKS, STATION WAGONS WSM
VOLVO 1944-1968 ALL MODELS WSM

VELOCEPRESS MOTORCYCLE BOOKS & MANUALS

AJS SINGLES 1955-65 350cc & 500cc (BOOK OF)
ARIEL 1939-1960 4 STROKE SINGLES (BOOK OF)
ARIEL LEADER & ARROW 1958-1964 (BOOK OF)
ARIEL MOTORCYCLES 1933-1951 WSM
ARIEL PREWAR MODELS 1932-1939 (BOOK OF)
BMW M/CYCLES R26 R27 (1956-1967) FACTORY WSM
BMW M/CYCLES R50 R50S R60 R69S (1955-1969) FACTORY WSM
BSA BANTAM (BOOK OF)
BSA ALL FOUR-STROKE SINGLES & V-TWINS 1936-1952 (BOOK OF)
BSA OHV & SV SINGLES - 250cc 1954-1970 (BOOK OF)
BSA OHV & SV SINGLES 1945-54 250-600cc (BOOK OF)
BSA OHV SINGLES 350 & 500cc 1955-1967 (BOOK OF)
BSA PRE-WAR MODELS TO 1939 (BOOK OF)
BSA TWINS 1948-1962 (BOOK OF)
BSA TWINS 1962-1969 (SECOND BOOK OF)
CATALOG OF BRITISH MOTORCYCLES (1951 MODELS)
DOUGLAS PRE-WAR ALL MODELS 1929-1939 (BOOK OF)
DOUGLAS POST-WAR ALL MODELS 1948-1957 FACTORY WSM
DUCATI 160cc, 250cc & 350cc OHC MODELS FACTORY WSM
HONDA 50 ALL MODELS UP TO 1970 INC MONKEY & TRAIL (BOOK OF)
HONDA 90 ALL MODELS UP TO 1966 (BOOK OF)
HONDA MOTORCYCLES 125-150 TWINS C/CS/CB/CA WSM
HONDA MOTORCYCLES 250-305 TWINS C/CS/CB WSM
HONDA MOTORCYCLES C100 SUPER CUB WSM
HONDA MOTORCYCLES C110 SPORT CUB 1962-1969 WSM
HONDA TWINS & SINGLES 50cc to 305cc 1960-1966 (BOOK OF)
HONDA TWINS ALL MODELS 125cc THRU 450cc UP TO 1968 (BOOK OF)
INDIAN PONYBIKE, BOY RACER & PAPOOSE ILL PARTS LIST & SALES LIT
LAMBRETTA ALL 125 & 150cc MODELS 1947-1957 (BOOK OF)
LAMBRETTA LI & TV MODELS 1957-1970 (SECOND BOOK OF)
MATCHLESS 350 & 500cc SINGLES 1945-1956 (BOOK OF)
MATCHLESS 350 & 500cc SINGLES 1955-1966 (BOOK OF)
NORTON 1938-1956 (BOOK OF)
NORTON DOMINATOR TWINS 1955-1965 (BOOK OF)
NORTON MODELS 19, 50 & ES2 1955-1963 (BOOK OF)
NORTON MOTORCYCLES 1957-1970 FACTORY WSM
NORTON PREWAR MODELS 1932-1939 (BOOK OF)
ROYAL ENFIELD SINGLES & V TWINS 1937-1953 (BOOK OF)
ROYAL ENFIELD 736cc INTERCEPTOR FACTORY WSM
ROYAL ENFIELD 250cc & 350cc SINGLES 1958-1966 (SECOND BOOK OF)
SUZUKI 50cc & 80cc UP TO 1966 (BOOK OF)
SUZUKI T10 1963-1967 FACTORY WSM
SUZUKI T20 & T200 1965-1969 FACTORY WSM
TRIUMPH PRE-WAR MOTORCYCLE 1935-1939 (BOOK OF)
TRIUMPH MOTORCYCLES 1937-1951 WSM
TRIUMPH MOTORCYCLES 1945-1955 FACTORY WSM
TRIUMPH TWINS 1956-1969 (BOOK OF)
VELOCETTE ALL SINGLES & TWINS 1925-1970 (BOOK OF)
VESPA 1951-1961 (BOOK OF)
VESPA 125 & 150cc & GS MODELS 1955-1963 (SECOND BOOK OF)
VESPA 90, 125 & 150cc 1963-1972 (THIRD BOOK OF)
VESPA GS & SS 1955-1968 (BOOK OF)
VINCENT MOTORCYCLES 1935-1955 WSM

www.VelocePress.com

Please check our website:

www.VelocePress.com

for a complete up-to-date list of available titles

www.ingramcontent.com/pod-product-compliance
Lightning Source LLC
Chambersburg PA
CBHW070602170426
43201CB00012B/1903